63

of the neoclassical theory of managerial remuneration," *Journal of Business Ethics*, February 1994. The total compensation included cash, benefits, perks, and long term incentives, for the CEOs of organizations with $ 250 million annual sales (same size companies).

6. Post-1991 figures for Germany are not comparable to pre-1991 figures, because Reunification brought along drastic changes in relevant parameters, such as labor supply, size of market, skill formation, work practices. German post-unification performance indicators would be "tainted" by the costs of absorption of an exogenous shock -- a shock not faced by the United States or Japan. Post-1991 figures for the U.S. are included not for comparative purposes, but in order to examine whether the changes in employment stability brought by Jointness are of a lasting or temporary nature.

7. This disadvantage, however, should not be exaggerated; such lack of mobility is also a predicament for tenured US professors.

8. Ben Hamper, *Rivethead: Tales form the Assembly Line* (New York: Warner Books, 1991), pp. 40 and 20.

9. The inappropriateness of the widely used measures of "productivity" as indicators of regime performance, as well as the strengths and weaknesses of our two indicators is discussed in Chapters 1 and 2.

10. Based on auto production figures from *Ward's Automotive Yearbook, 1994* (Southfield, MI.: Ward's Communications, 1994), p. 55.

11. For the derivation of auto reliability data see Appendix.

12. Ratings for earlier years are not available, because of luck of comparable models. For example, one of the highest-rated U.S. model for the period shown, Ford's Lincoln, was not produced before 1978.

13. On the relationship of the Democratic Party and the unions see Mike Davis, "The Barren Marriage of American Labour and the Democratic Party," *New Left Review*, 124 (November-December 1980). On the postwar evolution of the relationship between the party and the automobile union, see George Douglas Blackwood, *The United Automobile Workers of America 1935-1951*, Ph.D. Dissertation (Chicago: University of Chicago, 1951), pp. 392-395.

14. Evidently, we assume away generosity as a motive of capitalist behavior.

15. The Market Opinion Research, "Global Automotive Image Survey," as reported in PR Newswire, June 5, 1995.

16. Ample evidence against technology-based explanations of auto plant performance is provided by Womack et al. (1990) and Krafcik (1988).

17. The McKinsey Global Institute, *Manufacturing Productivity* (Washington, D.C.: McKinsey & Co., 1993). Baldwin and Clark (1994),

Womack et al. (1990) and Krafcik (1988) also dispute technology-driven explanations of US-Japan performance differentials.

18. See National Economic, Social, and Environmental Data Bank, *U.S. Industrial Outlook* (February 18, 1995), Chapter 35.

19. The McKinsey Global Institute, *Manufacturing Productivity* (Washington, D.C.: McKinsey & Co., 1993).

20. "If there was ever much reason to give credence to the notion of Japan, Inc., there is no reason to do so in the 1980s." T.J. Pempel, cited in Martin Kenney and Richard Florida, "Beyond Mass Production: Production and the Labor Process in Japan," *Politics and Society* (March 1988), p. 124. For a critical review of the "developmental state" and "corporatist" literatures of Japanese industrial success, see Masahiko Aoki, *Information, Incentives, and Bargaining in the Japanese Economy* (New York: Cambridge University Press, 1988), pp. 258-263.

21. The French state's intervention in industrial restructuring, according to W. Rand Smith, is of the "market-adapting" (as opposed to the more substantial, "market-modifying") type. "State, Labor, and Corporatism in France: Lessons of Industrial Restructuring," paper presented at the conference "A Century of Organized Labor in France: A Union Movement for the Twenty-First Century," Columbia University and New York University, February 9-10, 1996.

Appendix

1. CONSUMER REPORTS

The reliability rating of each automobile nameplate is the average of all the models of that nameplate, based on the Trouble Index of the annual Frequency-of-Repair Records compiled by *Consumer Reports*. The Trouble Index is a composite rating of the overall frequency and severity of reported problems in each model as compared with the average occurrence of the same problem in all models of that model year. The scores in the Trouble Index show how each model's overall reliability compares with the average model of the same age.

To earn a score of 4 or 2, a model had to differ from the model-year average by at least 15 %. To earn a score of 5 or 1, the model had to differ by at least 35 %. Otherwise, a car is rated as 3 for average.

The ratings were constructed on the basis of the proportion of owners who have reported serious problems for each trouble spot in each model year. The data came from readers' responses to Consumer Reports' Annual Questionnaires, covering experiences with hundreds of thousands of vehicles per year (550,000 responses in 1989). The data were standardized to minimize differences due to varied mileage.

Following is a key to the rating:

5 means a problem rate of 2.0 % or less.
4 means a problem rate of 2.0 % to 5.0 %.
3 means a problem rate of 5.0 % to 9.3 %.
2 means a problem rate of 9.3 % to 14.8 %.
1 means a problem rate of more than 14.8 %.

When we average the ratings of autos from one country without adjusting for the different market share of each model, we are allowing a certain distortion to enter into our results. The potential distortion that may result can be illustrated as follows. Let us assume that country A sells cars under only one nameplate, Z. Let us also assume that Z comes in two models, Z1 and Z2, with sales of Z1 making up 90% and of Z2 10% of total Z sales. Lastly, let us assume that the reported reliability rating of Z2 on a given year is 3, while that of Z2 is 5. Country A's auto reliability for that year would be recorded as "4" ("(3+5)/2"), whereas, from a different perspective, 90% of the cars sold by country A have receive a rating of 3. A more rigorous computation would include the share of sales of each model. In the example above the formula would be: "([3x90 + 5x10)/100]/)2 = 3.2". Unfortunately, as mentioned, such data are not available.

2. J.D. POWER & ASSOCIATES

Since 1985, JD Power's Vehicle Dependability Study surveys hundreds of thousands of buyers of new autos in the US about the frequency of repair of their autos **after 5 years of use**. It is based on the responses of some 22,000 owners annually, reporting on 31 nameplates.[1] The results of the survey are aggregated as the Vehicle Dependability Index (VDI), which reflects the totals of 12 separate problem areas. The problem areas, listed in order of their impact on satisfaction, are: engine, transmission, electrical and accessories, temperature control, brakes, squeaks and rattles, interior, exterior paint and moldings, steering and handling, body, water leaks and wind noise.

KEYNES'S
THIRD ALTERNATIVE?

NEW DIRECTIONS IN MODERN ECONOMICS SERIES
Series Editor: Malcolm C. Sawyer, Professor of Economics, University of York

New Directions in Modern Economics presents a challenge to orthodox economic thinking. It focuses on new ideas emanating from radical traditions including post-Keynesian, Kaleckian, neo-Ricardian and Marxian. The books in the series do not adhere rigidly to any single school of thought but share in common an attempt to present a positive alternative to the conventional wisdom.

The main emphasis of the series is on the development and application of new ideas to current problems in economic theory and economic policy. It will include new original contributions to theory, overviews of work in the radical tradition and the evaluation of alternative economic policies. Some books will be monographs whilst others will be suitable for adoption as texts. The series will highlight theoretical and policy issues common to all modern economies and is designed to appeal to economists throughout the world regardless of their country of origin.

Published titles

Post-Keynesian Monetary Economics: New Approaches to Financial Modelling
Edited by Philip Arestis

Keynes's Principle of Effective Demand
Edward J. Amadeo

New Directions in Post-Keynesian Economics
Edited by John Pheby

Theory and Policy in Political Economy: Essays in Pricing, Distribution and Growth
Edited by Philip Arestis and Yiannis Kitromilides

KEYNES'S THIRD ALTERNATIVE?

The Neo-Ricardian Keynesians and the Post Keynesians

AMITAVA KRISHNA DUTT

and

EDWARD J. AMADEO

Edward Elgar

Published by
Edward Elgar Publishing Limited
Gower House
Croft Road
Aldershot
Hants GU11 3HR
England

Edward Elgar Publishing Company
Old Post Road
Brookfield
Vermont 05036
USA

British Library Cataloguing in Publication Data
Dutt, Amitava Krishna, *1955–*
    Keynes's third alternative?: the neo-Ricardian Keynesians and
    the post Keynesians. – (New directions in modern economics).
    1. Economics. Theories of Keynes, John Maynard, 1883–1946
    I. Title II. Amadeo, Edward J. III. Series
    330.15'6

ISBN 1 85278 354 0

Printed in Great Britain by
Billing & Sons Ltd, Worcester

Contents

To Harolyn and Duda

Acknowledgements

We are grateful to Joaquim Andrade, Fernando Carvalho, Victoria Chick, Paul Davidson, William Darity, Sheila Dow, Geoff Harcourt, Murray Milgate, Malcolm Sawyer and Lance Taylor for comments and discussions. Special thanks go to Paul Davidson, Geoff Harcourt and Malcolm Sawyer for their detailed written comments and encouragement. We are also grateful to the participants of a session in the National Association of Centers of Graduate Studies in the Economics annual meetings, Brasilia, Brazil, in December 1986. We thank Marjula Maudgal for her assistance in preparing the index. We are grateful to Edward Elgar for his continuous encouragement. Finally, we wish to thank his editorial staff for seeing the book through to its completion.

The work for this book began when Dutt was visiting Pontifícia Universidade Católica, Rio de Janeiro in June–July 1986, and continued during Amadeo's visit to Florida International University in February–March 1988 and the University of Notre Dame in November 1988. We are grateful to the support of all three institutions. Dutt is also grateful to the Institute of Scholarship in the Liberal Arts at the University of Notre Dame for a summer research stipend.

E.J.A.
A.K.D.

1. Introduction

What is the central element of the so-called 'Keynesian Revolution'? Perhaps the vast majority of economists would answer this question by saying that there was never really a Keynesian Revolution. These economists would argue that Keynes, in the *General Theory*, provided a special case of the neoclassical model in which the money wage is rigid. Unemployment only results from the fact that the money wage rate is too high in relation to the price level and, therefore, firms are unable to employ all the workers willing to work at the prevailing real wage.

Not all economists, however, will give this answer. Two relatively small groups of non-mainstream Keynesians (or, to use Joan Robinson's term, non-bastard Keynesians) would deny that the cause of unemployment is the fact that wages are rigid. Post Keynesians would point to the role of uncertainty surrounding any act of decision making, to the role of money and to the effects of the irreversibility of time, in creating instability and in maintaining unemployment in the economy. Another group, the neo-Ricardian Keynesians, would argue that in a model with many commodities the rate of interest may not perform the role of equilibrating variable between saving and investment, a role which is filled by Keynes's multiplier mechanism: output would fall to a level below full employment to bring saving and investment to equality.

The objective of this book is to assess the ideas of these two schools of Keynesian economic thought as interpretations of Keynes's *General Theory*. We will examine their place in modern macroeconomics, analyse their approaches to the problems addressed by Keynes in the *General Theory*, com-

1

pare them, and try to ascertain to what extent they are truly in contradiction to each other.

We have two main reasons for studying the contributions of these two groups. First, we believe that they open up important areas in macroeconomic theory by diverting attention away from the issue as to whether or not wages are rigid. These areas include the importance of uncertainty, money and monetary institutions, and the role played by the interest rate as a macroeconomic equilibrating variable in capitalist economies. We believe that these areas deserve at least as much attention from macroeconomists as does wage rigidity. Second, the contributions of these groups have not been given much attention in the mainstream macroeconomic literature, and we believe that macroeconomics is the worse for this. The contributions have almost been shut out of macroeconomics textbooks,[1] and are seldom referred to in scholarly mainstream macroeconomics.[2] The reason for this neglect most commonly given is that they do not form a coherent theory.[3] Recently, their contributions have been receiving attention in some circles,[4] but these circles remain rather small; we believe that these schools should receive wider attention.

As for many other schools of thought, their contributors do not comprise homogeneous groups. This is especially true of the Post Keynesians. In our discussion we will not attempt a complete survey of the details regarding the contributions of each group,[5] but instead rely on our broad generalizations regarding the essence of each approach, rather like what Patinkin (1982) described as the 'central message' or the 'regression line'. This has the problem that it introduces a subjective element into our characterization of each school and of their major contributions. It also has the problem of what Pigou (1936) called 'lumping all . . . persons [in a school] together . . . [thereby enabling] the shortcomings of one to be attributed to all'. We try to overcome these problems by commenting on the work of several representative writers within each group, and by sometimes noting the differences in their emphases.

Since our purpose is to examine the contributions of these groups so far as they relate to the interpretation of the *General*

Theory, we do not examine the contributions of the group in a more general sense in a systematic manner. Our discussion will thus abstract from issues relating to the open economy and the dynamics of capital accumulation. This implies that we will not be able to address some issues to which both neo-Ricardians and Post Keynesians have devoted a considerable amount of attention.[6] The reason for these omissions is that the *General Theory* confines attention to the closed economy (aside from a few scattered comments) and assumes a given stock of capital. Given our purpose, even within the static, closed-economy setting we will be concerned only with contributions that have a direct bearing on interpreting the *General Theory*. Thus, except *en passant*, we will not be concerned with extensions of Keynes's work to cover such issues as imperfect competition, income distributional considerations, and details concerning the financial sector.[7]

We should also state at the outset that we use the term Post Keynesian in a sense somewhat different from the one often used. Dow (1985), Harcourt (1985, 1987 a,b) and Hamouda and Harcourt (1988) interpret the term much more broadly than we do.[8] Dow includes those we call neo-Ricardian Keynesians and Post Keynesians among those she calls the Post Keynesians, referring to them as two groups of Post Keynesians. Harcourt (1987a,b) and Hamouda (1988) cast an even wider net when they use the term Post Keynesian to include: those whose work follows a train deriving from Marshall following through Keynes; those following Marx through Sraffa, utilizing Keynes; those following Marx through Kalecki and Joan Robinson; and some outstanding individual figures such as Kaldor, Goodwin, Pasinetti, Shackle, and Godley and his colleagues. The first group of these, together with some of the contributions of the third group and individuals such as Shackle and Kaldor, we include among our Post Keynesians; the second group we call neo-Ricardian Keynesians.

Our justification for using the names the way we do follows from the objectives of the book. First, since one of the major themes in our analysis concerns the exploration of differences between the two groups of the non-mainstream Keynesians, we require different names for them; for lack of better names we use the terms neo-Ricardian Keynesians (given their self-acknowledged classical Ricardian roots) and Post Keynesians (following the name of the journal which is their major mouthpiece).[9] Dow and Hamouda and Harcourt were more interested in viewing the group as a whole and as an alternative to other schools; they were thus content with the portmanteau term Post Keynesians. Second, our Post Keynesian and neo-Ricardian Keynesians do not include all the contributions to what Harcourt and Hamouda call Post Keynesians because we have limited our attention to those who are concerned with closed-economy static issues which are directly relevant to interpreting Keynes's *General Theory*.

The rest of this book is organized as follows. Chapter 2 places the neo-Ricardian and Post Keynesians in the context of modern macroeconomic theory. Chapter 3 provides a background to the work of the two groups by examining some aspects of Keynes's method in the *General Theory*. Chapters 4 and 5 analyse respectively the central elements of the neo-Ricardian and Post Keynesian contributions. Chapter 6 compares the two sets of ideas and chapter 7 concludes.

NOTES

1. The influential textbook by Dornbusch and Fischer (1987) gives only half a page to the contributions of the Post Keynesians and does not mention the neo-Ricardians. Even the more eclectic work of Felderer and Homburg (1987) does not devote a whole page to them. See Colander (1986) for possible reasons why some contributions do not usually find their way into textbooks: their work cannot be (has not been?) put together in a simple, teachable model.
2. Solow (1979) mentions them in his survey of alternative macroeconomic theories, but ends with a negative assessment. Some sessions in the American Economic Association meetings have been devoted to these groups in the past [most notably the ones reported in the May 1980 and May 1984 issues of *American Economic Review*], but subsequent sessions are, despite popular attendance, not presented in the proceedings issue of the journal [see Davidson (1987a)].
3. Thus Dornbusch and Fischer (1987) write that 'Post Keynesian economics remains an eclectic collection of ideas, not a systematic challenge'. Felderer and Homburg (1987) write that they are 'somewhat

removed from prevailing orthodoxies and [do] not offer a coherent theory'. See also Solow (1979). Backhouse (1988, p. 40) suggests that these groups point out important issues often neglected in mainstream analysis; but 'whilst ... [they] ... may have many important and interesting things to say, they have not yet managed ... to provide a suitable alternative to the neoclassical research programme ...'

4. See, for example, Dow (1985), Harcourt (1987a,b) and Hamouda and Harcourt (1988).

5. A fairly exhaustive survey is available in Hamouda and Harcourt (1988). See also Harcourt (1985, 1987a,b).

6. See, for instance, Davidson (1982), Dow (1986-7) and Steedman (1979) for open economy issues, and Robinson (1956), Kahn (1959), Kaldor (1960), Davidson (1972) and Pasinetti (1981) for the analysis of growth.

7. We will be more specific in mentioning some of the more important omissions along these lines in what follows.

8. Earlier discussions used the term Post Keynesian in an even wider and more diluted sense. See for example Kurihara (1954).

9. We will return to this issue later.

2. Varieties of Modern Macroeconomics

INTRODUCTION

This chapter discusses the place of the Post Keynesians and the neo-Ricardian Keynesians in modern macroeconomic theory. Alternative approaches to macroeconomic theory will be described briefly in order to distinguish the two approaches with which we are concerned from the others. No attempt will be made at providing a complete coverage of the literature or in assessing the alternatives in detail. We will, where appropriate, use the standard textbook tool of the aggregate demand-aggregate supply (henceforth AD–AS) diagram (using unit price and output on the two axes) so as to present the analysis of the different schools using a common framework. We will also comment specifically on those aspects of the approaches which are particularly relevant to the issues raised later in this book.

The different approaches to macroeconomic theory that exist today can be classified into two broad groups according to whether or not they see the economy as always being in a position of full employment. We will discuss these two broad groups in the next two sections and compare them in the section, 'Comparisons and contrast'. The final section will consider Kalecki's theory, because of its closeness to the contributions of the Post Keynesian group.

THE CLASSICAL, MONETARIST AND RATIONAL EXPECTATIONS APPROACHES

In the first group can be placed the monetarist (labelled by Tobin (1980) and Hahn (1980) as the Mark I monetarists) and the rational expectations approaches. Both groups view wages and prices to be perfectly flexible, so that all markets clear through price variations. In particular, this implies that there can be no unemployment except for frictions and voluntary decisions (for searching or waiting). The two groups differ in their approach to the effectiveness of activist policy. The monetarist approach argues that monetary expansion can have temporary effects on output (as a result of expectational errors); longer-lasting expansion can only be achieved through continued monetary expansion which causes inflation to accelerate. The rational expectations approach, by assuming that agents form their expectations rationally (in the sense of Muth), shows that fiscal and monetary activity can have real effects only to the extent that the level of such activity is unanticipated by the public.[1]

The classical approach

These approaches can be seen as reincarnations of what Keynes called the classical model, and it is appropriate to start with that model as a point of departure. The analysis has the labour market at its core, and this market is examined using a demand curve and a supply curve of labour. Perfectly competitive,[2] profit-maximizing firms observe the wage and the price and demand labour up to the point at which the real wage is equal to the marginal product of labour; the demand curve for labour is thus given by the marginal product of labour. Formally, given capital and technology (so that we confine attention to the short period, ignoring accumulation of capital and technological change), the production function is

$$Y = F(N) \qquad (2.1)$$

where Y denotes the level of real output (and income) and N the level of employment. The profit-maximizing condition is given by

$$W/P = F'(N) \qquad (2.2)$$

where W is the money wage and P the price level.[3] Inverting this function gives the demand function for labour which is inverse since $F' < O$, due to diminishing returns:

$$N^d = N^d(W/P) \qquad (2.3)$$

Workers maximize their utility, given their preferences over income and leisure, with full knowledge of W and P; this implies

$$W/P = \Theta(N) \qquad (2.4)$$

where Θ is the marginal rate of substitution between income and leisure. This can be inverted to give the supply function for labour,

$$N^s = N^s(W/P) \qquad (2.5)$$

which we assume to have a positive derivative on the strength of a strong substitution effect. The demand and supply curves are drawn in Figure 2.1 as N^d and N^s. For a given P, perfect

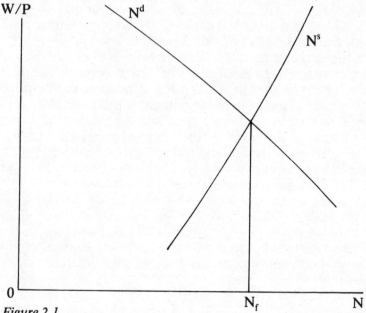

Figure 2.1

wage flexibility clears the labour market at N_f at the market-clearing real wage so that

$$N^d = N^s \qquad (2.6)$$

Apart from those frictionally unemployed, full employment prevails in the sense that all the labour supplied is employed. The resulting output in the economy, Y_f, is found from equation (2.1).

A version of Say's law implies that his output will be sold. Income is either consumed or saved. Fisherine savers maximize utility intertemporally and their saving is given by

$$S = S(i, Y) \qquad (2.7)$$

where S is real saving, i is the interest rate, and $S_i > 0$ is assumed on the basis of a strong substitution effect.[4] Investing firms maximize the present value of profits; under simple assumptions this implies equating the interest rate and the marginal product of capital. Notice that this implies that capital is interpreted as a homogeneous physical mass, so that we can find its marginal product. Notice also that the firm only cares about the technologically possible marginal product and is not concerned with what the market can take. Assuming diminishing marginal product of capital we obtain the investment function

$$I = I(i) \qquad (2.8)$$

where I is real investment, and $I' < 0$. With Y given at Y_f, we can draw the saving and investment functions in Figure 2.2. They represent, respectively, the supply and demand for loanable funds. Assuming perfect interest rate flexibility, the credit market will clear to equate saving and investment, so that

$$I = S \qquad (2.9)$$

Thus the part of output not demanded for consumption will be

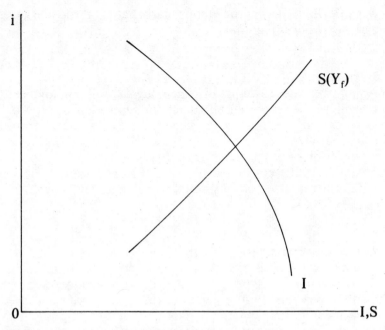

Figure 2.2

demanded for investment purposes and all the output will be sold.

The model so far can only determine the values of the real variables, and can solve for W only for the given P. Also, it should be noted that money has not made an appearance in the model. The monetary side of the economy is now appended to the model with a Fisherine quantity equation:

$$MV = PY \qquad (2.10)$$

where Y is determined at Y_f, V, the income-velocity of the circulation of money is given by the technology of money transactions and payments practices in the economy, and M is fixed by the monetary authorities. This equation thus solves for the price level, P. Note that money appears as a veil in this model; one need not even consider its existence to determine the 'real' part of the economy. Money simply exists as a medium of exchange to facilitate transactions; there is no other reason for holding it, and it gets its value (the inverse of P) due to the fact that the monetary authorities make it scarce by holding its supply constant.

The entire model can be represented using the aggregate demand (AD) and aggregate supply (AS) curves of Figure 2.3.

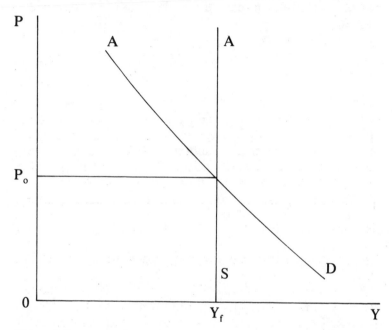

Figure 2.3

The AS curve follows from equations (2.1), (2.3), (2.5) and (2.6). The last three equations solve for N for a given P, this is also shown in Figure 2.1. Equation (2.1) then solves for Y at Y_f. For a different P these equations show that W adjusts to yield the same N and Y. Thus the AS curve is vertical at Y_f. The AD curve is given by equation (2.10), given M and V. Full employment equilibrium prevails at Y_f and the corresponding price level if P_o.

Equation (2.10) also implies that an exogenous change in M will result in an equiproportionate change in P without changing Y; this is the quantity theory of money. The model as written does not contain a transmission mechanism to show why an increase in money supply will increase the price level. However, several of them have been subsequently introduced. One is the real balance effect [see Pigou (1943) and Patinkin (1965)]. This can be incorporated into the model in a simple manner by introducing an additional variable in equation (2.7) and rewriting it as

$$S = S(i, Y, M/P) \qquad (2.11)$$

where the last partial is negative. This is due to the fact that if there is an increase in the real supply of money, individuals will want to spend their excess money balances on the purchases of goods, raising consumption and reducing S. There will be an excess demand for goods, P will rise, reducing M/P and eventually restoring equilibrium in the goods market. An additional mechanism, involving the asset demand for money, was also introduced following Keynes's analysis of money demand: excess money would imply an excess demand for bonds, reduce the i, and increase I, thereby increasing P. This can be formalized by rewriting equation (2.10) as

$$M/P = L(Y, i) \qquad (2.12)$$

where $L_y > 0$ due to a greater transactions demand for money and $L_i < 0$ because a higher interest rate makes wealth holders want to hold more interest yielding bonds rather than money. This approach departs from the approach of equation (2.10) by allowing the demand for money to depend on the interest rate, but does not necessarily imply a fundamentally different role for money. It can still be looked upon as being held to facilitate transactions and payments in the presence of transactions costs [see Baumol (1952)] with the interest rate appearing as the cost of holding money. And as before, the quantity of money is still determined by the monetary authorities.[5]

The monetarist and rational expectations approaches

The monetarist and rational expectations approaches can be seen as departing from the classical model in allowing for the fact that workers, who perhaps because they are generalists in consumption, cannot accurately predict the price level, and form an expectation of the price, P^e, when making their labour supply decision. Assuming everything else as before (price taking behaviour taking *expected* price as given, and utility-maximization) we must replace equation (2.4) by

$$W/P^e = \Theta(N) \tag{2.13}$$

which implies a labour supply function given by

$$N^s = N^s(W/P^e) \tag{2.14}$$

The behaviour of the firms is the same as before, so that we again have (2.2) and (2.3). Assuming perfect money-wage flexibility and labour-market clearing equations these equations imply

$$P = P^e \, \Theta(N)/F'(N) \tag{2.15}$$

which, using (2.1), implies

$$P = P^e \, f(Y) \tag{2.16}$$

where $f(Y) = \Theta(F^{-1}(Y))/F' \, (F^{-1}(Y))$ so that $f' > 0$. For a given P^e, this is represented as the AS curve of Figure 2.4. Y_f denotes the level of output at which $P^e = P$, so that from (2.15) Θ (N) $= F'(N)$, which we call *the* full employment level of output; this is also the Y_f point of the classical model where by definition we had $P = P^e$. Note that since the labour market clears at all points on the AS curve, any point on AS is a full employment point; points not at *the* full employment point either denote $P > P^e$ $(Y > Y_f)$ since workers are fooled into offering more labour because they expect the real wage (W/P^e) to be higher than what it is (W/P). The monetarist and rational expectations approaches part company regarding how workers form price expectations.

To develop the implications of this we need to complete the model by bringing in an AD curve. The simplest procedure would be to depict the demand side by equation (2.10), and draw the AD curve as a rectangular hyperbola as before. Monetarists and rational expectation theorists usually use a more complicated AD curve, derived from the neoclassical synthesis 'Keynesian' IS–LM apparatus. This takes investment to be given by equation (2.8), savings to be given by a simplification of (2.7):

$$S = S(Y) \qquad (2.17)$$

(although (2.7), or even the real-balance version (2.11) could just as well have been used). The IS curve shows combinations of Y and i which clear goods markets, that is, equation (2.9). The LM curve shows combinations of Y and i clearing the assets markets, for a given P (and M, which is fixed as before by the monetary authorities). These determine Y and i clearing the good and asset markets for the given P. A higher P implies that the LM curve moves, so that the markets-clearing Y is lower: a lower real supply of money implies an excess demand for money, a higher interest rate, and lower level of investment, a lower aggregate demand for the good, and a lower Y. The AD curve can then be taken as the downward-sloping relation which is thus obtained between P and Y, showing combinations of P and Y clearing the good and assets markets.

According to the monetarists, P^e can be thought of as being formed adaptively. An increase in money supply (starting from an initial position of 'long-run equilibrium' with $P = P^e$) would shift the AD curve in Figure 2.4 to $A'D'$. Since P^e is sticky, the economy would move in the short run from E_1 to E_2. This implies that P would exceed P^e, so that P^e would be pushed up adaptively, so that equation (2.16) implies that the AS curve would be shifted up gradually: the economy would move gradually following the arrows till a 'long-run equilibrium' at E_3, with $P = P^e$, is reached. Thus monetary policy can have a short-run real effect but not long-run ones.

Rational expectations theorists argue that adaptive expec-

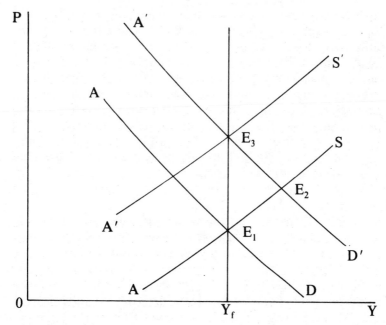

Figure 2.4

tation formation reflects irrational behaviour. They replace it by the hypothesis of rational expectations, according to which expectations are formed with full knowledge of the structure of the model, and the actual probability distributions of any stochastic factors that exist in the economy. Since for the time being we are abstracting from stochastic facts, we may assume that workers exactly calculate P^e from the model, so that when expected changes occur, they will expect the correct price immediately. Thus, if P^e is formed rationally, if the money supply change is expected (so that workers know that AD will be pushed to A'D'), they will immediately expect the price to be P so that the AS curve would instantly shift to A'S': there would be no real effect even in the short run. These rational expectations theorists complicate the analysis somewhat by allowing white noise random error terms to affect the positions of the AD and AS curves, so that output could deviate from Y_f due to deviations of actual (realized) AD and

AS curves from their expected positions. Individuals, in forming expectations, are assumed to know the true probability distributions of these error terms. The result is that only unanticipated changes in money supply (an unanticipated shift in the AD curve) can cause a deviation of Y from Y_f.

These approaches can be seen as theoretical challenges to Keynesian economics, which was concerned with an economy with unemployed labour. As mentioned above, they can also be seen as returns to what Keynes (JMK, VII) called the classical theory, modified to include expectational considerations – expectational errors in the monetarist approach, and stochastic elements and Muth-rational expectations in the rational expectations approach.[6]

They imply that any unemployment that exists is voluntary, since labour markets always clear. However, as Blinder (1987) sums it up, the question of involuntary unemployment is

a tough question to adjudicate on scientific grounds since the issue is largely definitional and, as Lewis Carroll pointed out, everybody is entitled to his own definitions. . . . However, a few pertinent facts should leaven the ideological debate. First, when the unemployment rate rises, it is layoffs, not quits, that are rising while consumption falls rather than rises – all of which are bad news for search theory. Second, real wage movements are close to a random walk – which is bad news for the intertemporal substitution approach. Third, unemployment is heavily concentrated among the long-term unemployed. . . . Fourth, unemployed workers normally accept their first job offer, and those who are looking for work spend on average only 4 hours per week on search activity.

These facts strongly undermine the claim that unemployment is purely voluntary.

KEYNESIAN APPROACHES

In the second group we have a variety of different approaches which allow unemployed labour to exist in the economy, at least for some length of time. Because of their consideration of unemployment, they can all be considered to be variants of Keynesian economics, and they are explicitly presented as such. They all have the common feature that they forsake

Say's law which makes the economy arrive at full employment, and follow Keynes (1936, p. 26) in saying that that law 'is not the true law relating aggregate demand and aggregate supply functions'.[7]

Wage-rigidity Keynesians

The most popular of these is the version of Keynes that has proliferated macroeconomic textbooks, and been called the neoclassical synthesis. The approach is depicted, in successive degrees of complexity, by the income–expenditure model (examining only on the goods market) following, for instance, Samuelson's *Economics*, the IS-LM model (examining goods and asset markets) following the work of Harrod (1937), Hicks (1937), Meade (1937) and Hansen (1949),[8] and by the aggregate-demand and aggregate-supply model (examining goods, assets and labour markets). This synthesis [see Modigliani (1944), for example] tried to show that unemployment equilibrium could occur only in the short run in which wages were rigid (either fixed or determined by a given function relating the money wage to the level of unemployment). In such equilibria, fiscal and monetary policy could work along Keynesian lines. But over time, with wages (either the fixed level or the function) moving down over time due to the pressure of unemployment, the economy would move to full-employment long-run equilibrium.

We turn again to the AD-AS framework, using Figure 2.5. The aggregate demand curve shows combinations of P and Y consistent with asset and goods market equilibria (determined by intersections of IS and LM curves at different levels of P, as before); this is the same as in a monetarist–rational expectations approach. We should note that the demand for money function can be modified to allow for asset holding behaviour in the presence of risk as shown by Tobin (1958), where asset holders choose between money and risky bonds (which have risky returns with a given probability distribution). For the simplest AS curve, assume a rigid money wage, W, in the short run. Profit maximizing, perfectly competitive firm behaviour implies

$$W/P = F'(N) \qquad (2.2)$$

Using (2.2) this implies that

$$P = W/F'(F(Y)) = W\, g(Y) \qquad (2.18)$$

where $g' > 0$. This gives the AS curve of Figure 2.5 for a given

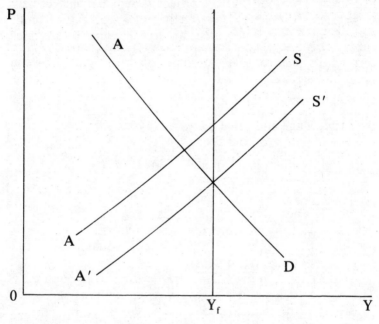

Figure 2.5

W. Rational expectations (actually perfect foresight) on the part of workers is assumed in this model, so that workers wish to supply an amount of labour given by $\Theta^{-1}(W/P)$ where Θ was defined above for equation (2.4). When this is equal to the amount that firms with to employ (given by $N^d = N^d(W/P) = F'^{-1}(W/P)$ from equation (2.3)) there will be full employment of labour, and output will be at Y_f. The AD and AS curves intersect to determine Y; given the money wage there is no reason for this intersection to occur at Y_f. The 'Keynesian' case occurs when the equilibrium Y is less than Y_f, so that equilibrium N is less than the one which clears the labour market. But as a result of unemployment, W would fall slowly over time due to a Phillips curve type effect; the AS curve would be pushed downward till, finally, 'long-run equilibrium' would occur when the AS curve is at $A'S'$.[9]

The key to the long-run full-employment outcome is obviously the downward-sloping and stable (in the face of wage reductions) AD curve. This downward slope is due to the so-called 'Keynes effect': price reductions increase the real supply of money, reduce the interest rate and expand output through its positive effect on investment demand. An economy starting from a long-run equilibrium position could raise its output only temporarily because of wage rigidity (so that the upward-rising AS curve would not move in the short run); over time wage and price increases (by moving the AS curve up) would reduce output because of the Keynes effect, returning the economy to full-employment equilibrium. To the Keynes effect one may add the real-balance effect according to which price reductions increase the real supply of money and thus increase the demand for goods as individuals and firms try to dispose of their excess money balances. Thus the economy would be Keynesian in the short run, but classical in the long run.

A second Keynesian approach, which Coddington (1983) calls 'reconstituted reductionism', grew out of the desire to form a bridge between neoclassical microeconomic theory (and Walrasian general equilibrium analysis) and the Keynesian approach just described. The work of Clower (1965), Leijonhufvud (1968), Malinvaud (1977) and others showed how with fixed prices (and wages) firms and households could be rationed in particular markets, and how when false trading occurs at the short side of the market and the effects could spill over into other markets, Keynesian unemployment and other types of situations could arise. The notions of 'effective' demands and supplies were coined in addition to the standard unconstrained 'notional' demands and supplies. The Keynesian region was characterized as having excess supplies (in the effective sense) in both goods and labour markets. Aside from other problems,[10] this approach takes wages and prices as given, without explanation.

A large literature has developed, however, which has tried to explain wage and price rigidity in terms of the neoclassical optimizing framework. For wage rigidity in the presence of unemployment, there have been theories of implicit contracts based on the risk-averse behaviour of workers, efficiency wage theories based on the firms' knowledge of the relationship between efficiency of workers and the wage, theories of union–firm bargaining, and insider–outsider models based on the monopoly power of insider–workers which induce firms to pay a non-market clearing wage.[11] For price rigidity, various types of models involving price-making behaviour by firms have been developed, of which the most popular have been models of monopolistic competition. An example of the models in this genre is Weitzman (1982), where price rigidity is explained endogenously in terms of profit-maximizing price setting by firms operating in a market with monopolistic competition and technology exhibiting economies of scale. There have also been attempts to show why behaviour that leads to sticky wages and prices may be not too far removed from rational behaviour and be 'near-rational' [see Akerlof and Yellen (1987)].

A common feature of the two types of approaches to Keynesian economics we have discussed, for which the theories just mentioned provide a theoretical rationale, is the assumption of wage rigidity.[12] This assumption has been a persistent theme in Keynesian economics. For example, the early formalizations of Keynes's model by Hicks (1937), Meade (1937) and Lange (1938) assumed that the money wage is fixed. Subsequently, Pigou (1943), Modigliani (1944), Haberler (1946a/b) and Patinkin (1965) tried to establish that under certain conditions (such as the absence of the liquidity trap or the presence of the real balance effect) the fixed money wage assumption was necessary for Keynesian unemployment; more recently, Kohn (1981) has made the claim in a stronger form, removing the qualifications made by them. Most macroeconomists (and most Keynesian macroeconomists) now seem to identify Keynesianism with the fixed money-wage assumption (and we will therefore call this approach mainstream Keynesianism). As illustrations we may cite the recent overview of macroeconomics made by Modigliani (1986), Kohn's (1986) evaluation of Keynes's *General Theory* analysis, and McCallum's (1987) statement that '[t]he key characteristic of Keynesian macroeconomics that distinguishes it from Classical theory is a postulated stickiness in some nominal price . . .'

This view of Keynesian economics seems to suggest that Keynes did not make a fundamental theoretical advance over those he described as the classical economists. A review of the work of these classical economists seems to show that Keynes was only repeating their conclusions – that wage rigidity causes unemployment and wage flexibility will erase unemployment.[13] The simple classical model with a quantity equation given by equation (2.10), a demand curve for labour (the marginal product curve), a supply curve for labour, and a given money wage, can be depicted by an aggregate demand (rectangular hyperbola) curve and an (upward-rising) aggregate supply curve in price-output space, yielding equilibrium at less-than-full-employment output. The qualification that his predecessors had not analysed in detail the implications of wage rigidity for the goods market in terms of aggregate demand and supply analysis and the multiplier does not detract from the force of this argument.

Post Keynesians and neo-Ricardian Keynesians

The Keynesians with whom we are concerned in this book can be sharply distinguished from these other varieties of Keynesians in that they do not view Keynes's analysis, or the existence of unemployment, as requiring wage rigidity.

The Post Keynesians emphasize Keynes's contributions on uncertainty, the properties of money, and the role of historical time. They emphasize the role of uncertainty surrounding any act of decision making. In a world of uncertainty money plays a major role in protecting agents against the effects of the irreversibility of time. When uncertainty increases agents prefer to hold liquid assets (money being a liquid asset *par excellence*). If agents are able to hold money rather than use their income to buy goods, there is a permanent threat that the income–expenditure circuit will be interrupted, thus causing unemployment.

The Post Keynesians depart from the type of equilibrium models used by the Keynesians discussed above, dismissing these models as an inadequate basis on which to study the functioning of monetary production economies. To them, the argument that the rigidity of the money wage is the cause of unemployment does not hold water, since it is 'proved' in terms of a model which ignores the essential aspects of Keynes's theoretical contributions. Their equilibrium notion does not take into account the fact that agents make decisions when time flows from an irreversible past to an uncertain future, and does not take into account the real role of money.

The neo-Ricardian Keynesians argue that in a model with many commodities the rate of interest may not perform the role of equilibrating variable between saving and investment. That is why the neoclassical theory of employment is flawed. Keynes's multiplier mechanism provides a consistent theory of the adjustment of saving and investment, and the level of output. According to this mechanism, saving adjusts to investment through changes in the levels of income, output and employment. The level of employment determined by the equilibrium between saving and investment will correspond to full employment only by coincidence.

The failure of the interest rate mechanism due to the heterogeneity of capital goods, and not the rigidity of the money wage, is the cause of unemployment. Neo-Ricardians [see, for example, Eatwell and Milgate (1983)] have carefully tried to distinguish their approach from those that they call 'imperfectionists', that is, those who believe that the economy would tend to full employment were it not prevented in doing so by the existence of certain rigidities, frictions or imperfections.

COMPARISONS AND CONTRASTS

This brief discussion of alternative approaches to macroeconomic theory shows that there are important differences between the monetarist (including rational expectations approaches) and the Keynesian approaches. The former believe that free markets result in full employment and that there is no need for active policy intervention (and in fact that such intervention is undesirable), while the latter view the free market as not resulting in full employment, so that active policy has a role to play.

However, there are sharp differences within the Keynesian approaches as well. The mainstream approaches view economies basically in the same way as do monetarists (and this is reflected by the similarity of their models) but believe that imperfections and rigidities (primarily that of the money wage) result in unemployment. If these rigidities could be removed, the economy would be taken to full employment. While nothing in their analysis necessarily implies that the rigidities are in fact removable, this approach naturally leads one to ask how they can be removed, and to believe that they do not operate in the long run. The Post Keynesians and neo-Ricardians, on the other hand, see unemployment as arising from more 'fundamental' characteristics of capitalist economies, so that attention shifts away from removing rigidities in the system to trying to understand the role of these fundamental characteristics.[14] The analytical approaches of the schools are also very different from the monetarists and wage-rigidity Keynesians. The latter use the IS–LM and similar models, arguing basically about whether rigidities exist, and about what the elasticities of different functions are. The former either use different types of models or shy away from models altogether. One important implication of the similar approach of the latter is that the analysis of long-run dynamics is carried on basically the same way for the monetarists and mainstream Keynesians, that is, with the use of the neoclassical growth models. Even if wages are rigid in the short run, so that unemployment can exist, in the long run both approaches assume full employment. For the Post Keynesians and the neo-Ricardians, long-run analysis does not assume full-employment growth.

A NOTE ON KALECKI

In this chapter we have discussed several different approaches to macroeconomic theory in order to compare the Post Keynesians and neo-Ricardians to alternative approaches. In doing so, however, we have not discussed *all* alternative approaches. In particular, we have not discussed the approach deveoped by Kalecki (1971) which has spawned a large literature synthesizing different strands of Marxian and structuralist thinking.[15]

It is commonly acknowledged that Kalecki developed the macroeconomic theory of demand-determined equilibrium independently and prior to Keynes. Some would even say that by introducing imperfect competition, allowing for excess capacity utilization, emphasizing the different spending patterns by different classes, and analysing explicitly cyclical issues, his theory was superior to Keynes's.

This book is concerned with the neo-Ricardian Keynesian and Post Keynesian interpretations of Keynes's *General Theory*, not with Kalecki's analysis. However, many Post Keynesians (and some other Keynesians as well) have borrowed from Kalecki's work (especially those parts on imperfect competition, income distribution, and the role of banks), which means that we will be making some passing references to his work in what follows. It is therefore useful to present a brief account of some features of Kalecki's macroanalysis, although abstracting from the dynamic (cyclical) features of his analysis.[16]

Kalecki assumes that firms set their price as a markup on prime costs (labour costs).[17] Assuming a fixed labour–output ratio given by a, this implies that the price is determined by

$$P = (1+z)Wa \qquad (2.19)$$

where z, the markup, is determined by factors such as the degree of industrial concentration, the strength of unions, etc., subsumed by Kalecki in what he called the degree of monopoly.[18] The firms operate with excess capacity. This equation gives us the horizontal AS curve of Figure 2.6. Assume that workers consume all their income and capitalists (who earn markup income) save a constant fraction, s, of their profits. For simplicity (primarily to abstract from cyclical and growth issues) assume that real investment, I, is given. Saving–investment equality (required for goods-market clearing) then implies that

$$Y = I/[sz/(1+z)] \qquad (2.20)$$

which is seen to be independant of P; this gives the vertical AD curve of Figure 2.6. Macroeconomic equilibrium (somewhat

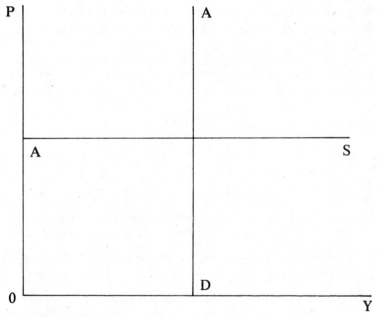

Figure 2.6

unnecessarily, perhaps) is shown to be given at the intersection of the AD and AS curves. This output level is assumed to be one which does not employ the total supply of labour, so that there is unemployment.

Note that in this model a fall in the money wage due to unemployment would, with given z and a, reduce P equiproportionately. The AS curve would shift down over time, but not increase Y which would be determined by (2.8). If the fall in W, however, did not result in an equiproportionate fall in P, z would increase, implying, by equation (2.8), a fall in Y and a leftward shift in the AD curve. Unemployment would therefore increase. It could be objected that all this assumes away the Keynes effect (that is the effect on I through the interest rate mechanism) and the real-balance effect (which could reduce s), both of which would tend to push up Y as a result of deflation. However, Kalecki had stories to tell on why these effects would not remove unemployment. Because of their close similarity with Post Keynesian ideas, however, the discussion of Kalecki's views on these issues is postponed till chapter 5.

One feature of Kalecki's short-run analysis that we should mention is that it was also valid for the longer run. The behaviour of the economy was in the long run an average of its behaviour in the short run, so that no analysis of the latter was valid without an examination of the former.

NOTES

1. The rational-expectations policy ineffectiveness result can also be established in models in which the labour market does not clear. See, for example, Fischer (1977). Here the crucial assumption is that expected inflation is translated, one for one, into nominal wage changes. It should also be noted that tax policy changes can have real effects in rational-expectations models due to supply effects, unless individuals discount them by taking into account their consequences for tax changes in the future.
2. This assumption of perfect competition implying, among other things, atomistic behaviour amongst firms, is different from the notion of competition used in Smith, Ricardo and Marx, the real classical economists. The latter used the term to refer to the mobility of capital between different sectors of the economy, and this did not necessarily require the assumption of price-taking behaviour. See Dutt (1988). The neo-Ricardian Keynesians, as will be clear from the discussion in

chapter 4, use the classical, and not the atomistic notion of competition.

3. We are implicitly assuming that all firms are identical, and using the concept of the representative firm. Similar assumptions will be made for simplicity, to sidestep the problems of aggregation, except where explicitly noted to the contrary.

4. Since we abstract from inflation or its expectation, this can be interpreted as a real or nominal one; the classical model takes it to be the real interest rate.

5. Solving for the model graphically now becomes a little more complicated. Equations (2.8), (2.9) and (2.11) yield a goods-market equilibrium schedule in P,i space for given Y at Y_f. Equation (2.12) yields an asset-market equilibrium schedule in the same space. They jointly determine i and P. See, for example, Tobin (1980). An alternative presentation would derive an AD curve from this. The diagram just described assumes that Y is at Y_f. Now interpret this diagram as solving for P for an arbitrary Y. For different levels of Y we would get different curves and correspondingly different levels of P at their intersection. This would provide us with a downward-sloping AD curve. A vertical AS curve at Y_f could then be combined with it to determine Y and P. Note that this model still implies full-employment equilibrium and the quantity theory of money.

6. We will refer to Keynes's work using JMK and the volume number in the Collected Works, but all other references will be by name and date of publication.

7. Keynes (JMK, VII, p. 26) writes that 'Say's law, that the aggregate demand price of output as a whole is equal to its aggregate supply price for all volumes of output, is equivalent to the proposition that there is no obstacle to full employment'. This is not quite correct, since wage rigidity and imperfect competition in the product market [see Weitzman (1982)] can cause unemployment even with identical aggregate supply and demand curves, and monetarist and rational expectations approaches make the economy arrive at full employment even though they distinguish between aggregate demand and aggregate supply curves. Here we interpret Say's law as stating that the economy arrives at full employment, and its denial as stating that equilibrium can be reached at less than full employment due to the lack of demand (even if this is caused by wage rigidity). In this sense all varieties of Keynesianism can be said to forsake Say's law, although with some other definition of Say's law this statement does not hold true. See, for example, Davidson (1984) for a discussion of the interpretation of Say's law made by Keynes, regarding the identity of the aggregate supply and demand curves.

8. See Young (1987) for a discussion of the development of the IS-LM approach showing the importance of the work of Harrod and Meade (in addition to Hicks's) in its early development.

9. This analysis does not require a fixed W in the short run; we could have assumed a positive relation between W and N fixed in the short run, and assume that this relation moves through time due to Phillips-type effects. Notice also the different definition of the long run, and conceptions of long-run equilibrium, in this approach and the monetarist one.

10. These include the inconsistency between perfect competition and sales constraints, and their faithfulness to Keynes's analysis, which allowed goods markets to clear. See, for example, Hahn (1977). See also Kahn (1977) and Davidson (1984).

11. See Solow (1979) for an excellent, though dated, review of the literature, Azariadis (1975) for implicit contracts theory, Akerlof and Yellen (1986) for a survey and a sample of papers on efficiency wage theories, McDonald and Solow (1981) for bargaining theory, and Lindbeck and Snower (1987) for insider-outsider and efficiency wage models. Trevithick (1976) has also examined Keynes's own explanation of wage rigidity in terms of workers' concern over their relative pay.

12. At least one of the contributions, namely that of Weitzman (1982), explicitly states that it does not require wage rigidity to show that unemployment exists in the economy. When the money wage falls, the price level falls proportionately, leaving employment unaffected. However, this model assumes away the Keynes effect by leaving out investment from the analysis and also abstracts from real balance effects. When Weitzman (1985) works with a similar model which introduces the real balance effect, he does find that wage-flexibility in the long run results in full employment. There have also been other 'Keynesian' contributions which do not depend on wage rigidity. Diamond's (1984) search model is an example, but while it shows the effectiveness of policy and a market failure, it does not allow for involuntary unemployment, only 'wait' or 'search' unemployment.

13. See, for example, Marshall (1920), Pigou (1927, 1933), and Schlesinger (1956). Modern-day monetarist and rational expectations approaches which do not admit of wage rigidities can thus be said to be closer to Keynes's classical economists than the pre-Keynesians for whom Keynes had used the term.

14. These approaches are thus closer to the monetarists in minimizing the role of rigidities and distortions, although for different reasons. To the monetarists, they are empirically unimportant, but to the Post Keynesians and neo-Ricardians, they are theoretically unimportant. However, while the former approaches would be undermined by the existence of rigidities, the latter would not.

15. See, for example, Taylor (1983) and Bhaduri (1986).

16. For a more detailed discussion of Kalecki's theories see Sawyer (1985).

17. We abstract entirely from raw material-producing sectors where the price is demand-determined. See Kreisler (1987) for a detailed discussion of Kalecki's pricing theory.

18. This equation departs from the perfectly competitive assumptions made in the AD-AS models discussed so far, and also does not necessarily imply any optimizing behaviour on the part of firms.

3. Keynes's Method in the General Theory

INTRODUCTION

The recent controversies over the *General Theory* between neo-Ricardians and Post Keynesians are closely associated with Keynes's method of analysis. In this chapter we examine Keynes's method in the *General Theory* in order to compare the two groups of economists, and assess some of the issues discussed in these controversies. Our interpretation is that Keynes made use of three models in the book. The first model refers to the determination of output and employment, given producers' expectations, and once they are fixed, the determination of the price level in the (Marshallian) market period. The second model is essentially a formal model providing a clear exposition of Keynes's central ideas and serving as a benchmark for further discussions. The third model is based on the structure of the second one but it is less formal in the sense that it discusses matters which would be much more difficult to put in mathematical language.

The second model is the short-period equilibrium model: it is designed to explain the equilibrium configuration of the endogenous variables given the values of the exogenous variables and the functional relations of the system.[1] The first model focuses on market-period equilibrium positions and the transition paths between two short-period equilibrium positions. We shall refer to it as the market-period model. The third model discusses the determinants of (and the effects of) changes in the 'givens' of the model and shall be referred to as the historical model. From our point of view, it is important to distinguish between the three models for a proper understand-

30

ing of Keynes's message in the *General Theory*, because they focus on different aspects of the theory of employment and the price level.

In this chapter we shall discuss the relation between the three models. We shall argue that, in a sense, the second model can be seen as a development of the first, and the third as a development of the second. In this way the three models together form a coherent *theory* of employment and the price level. We shall suggest that whereas the neo-Ricardian interpretation of Keynes's economics focuses on the equilibrium model, the Post Keynesian approach emphasizes the two other models.[2]

THE MARKET-PERIOD MODEL

The origin of the principle of effective demand as presented in the *General Theory* is to be found in Keynes's 1930 book, *A Treatise on Money*.[3] In the theoretical chapters of the *Treatise* (Books III and IV), Keynes develops his fundamental equations. With these equations Keynes discusses the determination of the price level in a static model (in which the level of output is given), and the determination of the levels of price, output and employment over a sequence of 'production periods'. The dynamic model of the *Treatise* is revised and expanded in the drafts of the *General Theory*, and provides the basis for the first model of the 1936 book – the market-period model.

The market-period model is discussed in chapters 3, 5, 7 and 10 of the *General Theory*. Producers' short-period expectations play a central part in the determination of output and employment.[4] Given the price of the factors of production, producers are assumed to maximize their expected profits (or the excess of the sales proceeds over variable costs), and thus determine the levels of output and employment.

If labour is the only variable input, given the wage rate (W), the expected price (P^e) and the production function $Y = F(N)$,[5] firms are assumed to maximize ($P^e Y - WN$) subject to the technological constraint, that is, the production function.

The levels of employment and output resulting from this maximization process (Y* and N*, respectively) must satisfy the following condition: $W/P^e = F'(N^*)$, that is, the expected real wage must be equal to the marginal product of labour. Hence the determination of the level of employment in the market-period model is based on producers' expectations concerning the demand for their products and the cost structure.

Producers form their short-period expectations based on past experience and the new information available to them in the beginning of the period. Unexpected changes in aggregate demand (due to changes in the government fiscal policy for example) will affect the demand for goods for each individual industry. If producers' expectations concerning the demand for their product are incorrect, either prices or the level of inventories will have to adjust once the finished output reaches the market.[6] Assuming that only prices change, the difference between the realized or market price and the expected price gives rise to what Keynes in his *Treatise on Money* called 'windfall profits or losses'. Formally these can be represented by the following equation:

$$Q_t = [P_t - P^e_t]Y_t^*$$

where P is the market price and subscript t dates the market period. Producers take the change in prices (or inventories) as relevant information for the determination of the expected sales proceeds in the next period. Here we can quote Keynes:

The *actually realized* results of the production and sale of output will only be relevant to employment in so far as they cause a modification of subsequent expectations . . . Thus, on each and every occasion . . . the decision will be made . . . in the light of the *current* expectations of *prospective* costs and sale-proceeds. (JMK, VII, p. 47)

An unforeseen change in investment demand, for example, and the resulting change in the output of the capital goods sector will probably create a discrepancy between the expected and actual prices, and affect the levels of output and employment in the consumption goods sector over a *sequence* of production periods:

a *change* in expectations . . . will only produce its full effect on employment over a considerable period. The change in employment due to a change in expectations will not be the same on the second day after the change as on the first, or the same on the third day as on the second and so on, even though there be no further change in expectations. (JMK, VII, pp. 47–8)

Thus, given a once and for all change in the exogenous determinants of aggregate demand, the process of trial-and-error through which producers decide on the levels of employment and output will, together with other adjustment mechanisms such as the inducement to consume, determine the path of the system until a new equilibrium is reached.[7] This process we see as the embryo of the multiplier mechanism – a mechanism which is central for the development of the equilibrium model.[8]

THE SHORT-PERIOD EQUILIBRIUM MODEL

In the equilibrium model, short-period expectations (that is, expectations over the production period) are not important, and therefore can be neglected. In fact, Keynes assumes that producers' expectations over the multiplier process are never mistaken. The reason for this assumption is that short-period expectations are formed through an almost continuous process of trial-and-error in which the most recent events play an important part. Therefore, the changes in the economic environment from one period to the next are not large and frequent, which means that on average the path of the system is not greatly affected by short-period expectations. Thus Keynes notes that

it will often be safe to omit express reference to short-term expectations, in view of the fact that in practice the process of revision of short-term expectations is a gradual and continuous one, carried on largely in the light of realized results . . . (JMK, VII, pp. 50–1)

It is important to note that this passage refers to short-term expectations only, and the omission of expectations should not be extended to the long-term expectations – '[e]xpress reference to current long-term expectations can seldomly be avoided' (JMK, VII, p. 50).[9] Whereas short-period expectations affect producers' decisions to produce and employ, and can be checked and revised at very short intervals, long-period expectations concern decisions to invest. The formation and revision of long-period expectations have completely different characteristics. They refer to long intervals of calendar time, and therefore cannot be compared in any meaningful sense with the recent experience. That is, the events in the recent past are not such a good approximation of the events and the environment in the future. Therefore, investors can rely only to a certain extent on the current information concerning the market conditions, and their 'animal spirits'.

In the equilibrium model, therefore, (only) short-period expectations are assumed to be continuously fulfilled. In his 1937 lecture notes, Keynes argues that mistaken short-period expectations are not really relevant for the determination of the short-period equilibrium position:

I begun . . . by regarding [the difference between expected and actual demand] as important. But eventually I felt it to be of secondary importance, emphasis on it obscuring the real argument. For the theory of effective demand is substantially the same if we assume that short-period expectations are always fulfilled. (JMK, XIV, p. 181)

The equilibrium model is stated in chapter 18 of the *General Theory*.[10] The causal relationship between the independent and dependent variables is quite clearly described in this chapter. In what follows we reproduce passages of the chapter:

There will be an inducement to push the rate of new investment to the point which forces the supply-price of each type of capital asset to a figure which, taken in conjunction with its prospective yield, brings the marginal efficiency of capital in general to approximate equality with the rate of interest.

But an increase (or decrease) in the rate of investment will have to carry with it an increase (or decrease) in the rate of consumption . . . changes in the rate of consumption are, in general, *in the same direction* (though smaller in amount) as changes in the rate of income . . .

Finally, if we assume . . . that the employment multiplier is equal to the investment multiplier, we can . . . infer the increment of employment. (JMK, VII, p. 248)

Based on the equilibrium model, the principle of effective demand can be enunciated in its most simple and fundamental version: the state of liquidity preference, the quantity of money and the long-period expectations determine the volume of investment which, together with the multiplier mechanism, determines the equilibrium levels of employment, income and saving. The multiplier mechanism brings about the gradual adjustment of income and saving to the level of investment. The role of income (rather than the interest rate) as the equilibrating factor between investment and saving is what makes the adjustment process revolutionary in terms of the traditional theory of employment and the price level in the 1920s and 30s.

The conclusions associated with the equilibrium model are obviously conditional and partial: they assume that there are certain variables which do not depend on the workings of the system, and more than that, are fixed until the adjustment process has come to an end. For this reason the model cannot be ascribed any descriptive role; it is no more than an analytical tool which serves the purpose of organizing our ideas. The advantage of the model is that its results are logically necessary (since they come from a mathematical model), and therefore quite clear and definite.

The aim of the traditional approach to monetary theory before the *General Theory* was published was to explain the causes of cycles and fluctuations around a norm characterized by the full employment of resources and, in particular, the available labour. In terms of logically necessary relations, Keynes developed a model in which the equilibrium or norm was no longer characterized by the full employment of labour or the full utilization of capacity. In his comments on the *General Theory*, Robertson seems to admit that Keynes's analysis was different from the traditional credit cycle theories:

I take this proposition [on the endemic nature of unemployment] to be the real *differentia* of the book, marking it off from your own *Treatise* as well as from most of the other literature of disequilibrium, which runs, as the *Treatise* did, in terms of fluctuations around a norm and not of chronic failure to get up to a norm. (JMK, XIII, p. 500)

As we shall note in the following section, Keynes did not neglect the study of fluctuations or cycles. However he did ascribe great importance to the conclusions associated with the equilibrium model in the *General Theory*. Certainly the main conclusion is the possibility of equilibrium *cum* unemployment:

the economic system may find itself in stable equilibrium with N [employment] at a level below full employment, namely at the level given by the intersection of the aggregate demand function and the aggregate supply function. (JMK, VII, p. 30)

We may finally turn to the third model which, as noted already, can be seen as a step forward in comparison with the equilibrium model.

THE HISTORICAL MODEL

The controversies over the *General Theory* usually refer to the appropriateness of taking certain variables as given or independent from the workings of the system, or to the ultimate meaning ascribed by Keynes to the notions of 'given' and 'independent'. One possible way to discuss these controversies is by isolating the short-period equilibrium model from the other two models. In the latter, not only do short-term expectations play a part in the analysis (market-period model) but also the determinants of (and effects of changes in) the independent variables are discussed (historical model). The equilibrium model provides a clear-cut exposition of the determinants of income and employment as well as a benchmark for discussing the other two models. It can also be seen as the outcome of a sequence of market-period equilibrium positions.

The repercussions between the dependent and independent variables during the workings of the adjustment process as well as the causes of alterations in the value of the independent variables and given factors are associated in the *General Theory* with the 'facts of experience [which] do not follow from logical necessity' (JMK, VII, p. 250). In the book Keynes distinguishes between the logically necessary relations and those which depend on particular or ephemeral circumstances and, therefore, for the purpose of his analysis, can *noi* be generalized. In proceeding this way, he argued as follows:

our analysis . . . provide[s] ourselves with an organized and orderly method of thinking out particular problems; and, after we have reached a provisional conclusion by isolating the complicating factors one by one, we then have to go back on ourselves and allow . . . for the probable interactions of the factors amongst themselves. This is the nature of economic thinking. (JMK, VII, p. 297)

In the historical model feedback effects between the determinate variables and the determinants, and alterations of the factors determining the independent variables are considered. Changes in long-period expectations for example will affect not only the prospective yield of capital goods but also the state of liquidity preference, and therefore the rate of interest. A situation of great uncertainty can lead to an increase in liquidity preference and also a reduction in the propensity to invest. A situation of persistent unemployment may lead to reductions in money wages with multiple effects on the determinants of aggregate demand.[11] Changes in the level of employment will affect the transaction demand for money and if the quantity of money remains constant, this will have an effect on the rate of interest.[12] An increase in investment demand will eventually affect the stock of capital with obvious repercussions on the marginal efficiency of capital and the inducement to invest.

These are all direct or repercussion effects which can be studied but not with the degree of precision of the equilibrium model. In particular, when repercussion effects are taken into account in an equilibrium model, the initial notion of equilibrium will change since the givens and functional relations of the system will be different. Furthermore, some of the repercussion effects will have a multiple or non-systematic influence on the equilibrium configuration since the value of several independent variables may be affected in complex ways, thus rendering the results of the model ambiguous.

Thus, the equilibrium model provides a clear-cut relationship between the independent and dependent variables of the system. Repercussion effects (that is, feedback effects between the dependent and independent variables) establish new equilibrium positions each time the value of an independent variable changes. It is as if a vector of values A of the independent variables would lead to a vector of values B of the dependent variables which, in turn, would lead to a vector A' of the independent variables, and so on. The question which then arises refers to the effect of these repercussions on the trajectory of the system over time: do they lead to violent changes in prices and employment, or is there a regular cyclical movement around a norm established by given values of the more stable independent variables? The answer to this question depends very much on the functional relationships of the system, or in other words, the value of the parameters which relate changes in dependent and independent variables. This is an issue which permeates the controversy between Keynesians of different strands, and in particular Post Keynesians and neo-Ricardians. It was indeed an issue which Keynes considered in the *General Theory*:

Fluctuations may start briskly but seem to wear themselves out before they have proceeded to great extremes, and an intermediate situation which is neither desperate nor satisfactory is our normal lot. . . .

Now, since these facts of experience do not follow of logical necessity, one must suppose that the environment and the psychological propensities of the modern world must be of such character as to produce these results. (JMK, VII, p. 250)

Hence, continues Keynes, it is 'useful to consider what hypothetical psychological propensities would lead to a stable system'. He then goes on to examine the values of four functional relations of the short-period equilibrium model, namely, the propensity to consume, the schedule of marginal efficiency of capital, the response of money wages to changes in employment, and the effect of changes in the stock of capital on the prospective yield of investment.

As for the propensity to consume, Keynes suggests that it is smaller than one, and therefore that the multiplier is greater than one, but not very large. Experience seems to show that this is the case. Otherwise, that is if the propensity to consume was equal to one, given an increase in investment, we would observe a cumulative increase in effective demand until the point at which full employment (or full capacity) necessarily would be reached. A fall in investment, on the other hand, would lead to a situation of zero-employment. However, 'experience shows that we are generally in an intermediate position' (JMK, VII, p. 252).

Changes in long-period expectations or the rate of interest do not lead to great changes in the rate of investment because, unless there is a considerable degree of excess capacity in the capital goods sector, the increase in demand will be matched by an increase in the supply price of capital goods, thus tending to limit the expansion of investment.

Changes in employment are not associated with great changes in money-wages and therefore prices. Keynes suggests that 'workers will not seek a much greater money-wage when employment increases or allow a very great reduction rather than suffer any unemployment at all' (JMK, VII, p. 253). The main argument here is associated with Keynes's notion that workers in any industry will try to maintain stable the relation between their money-wages and the wages paid in other industries.[13]

Finally, Keynes refers to the effect of changes in the marginal efficiency of capital as the stock of capital changes. An increase in the stock of a certain type of capital tends to reduce the expected yield of that particular type of capital, thus reducing the inducement to invest. On the other hand, as a particular type of capital wears out, given the conditions of demand for the output produced with it, its prospective yield will tend to increase. Thus there is a built-in stabilizer element in the inducement to invest which lends some stability to the system.

In sum, it would seem reasonable to argue that Keynes's three models, together with the stabilizing elements in the main relations of the short-period model and in the repercussion effects, give rise to a theoretical system which is capable of explaining both changes in the norm around which the economy gravitates, as well as the causes of such fluctuations. In fact Keynes directed his efforts to develop a theory which could provide an explanation for

an outstanding characteristic of the economy system in which we live [namely] that, whilst it is subject to severe fluctuations . . . it is not violently unstable [and it] seems capable of remaining in a chronic condition of subnormal activity for a considerable period . . . (JMK, VII, p. 249)

CONCLUDING REMARKS

Each of the models discussed here has its advantages and disadvantages. The short-period equilibrium model provides definite results; the market-period model is particularly well suited for the analysis of adjustment processes; and the historical model essentially makes the equilibrium model more inclusive and richer. On the other hand, the market-period and historical models depend too much on expectations (short and long) and since we know very little about how expectations are formed, especially in situations involving change, the analysis is bound to be tentative.

It is our suggestion that the two groups of economists being analysed in this book can be distinguished from one another in terms of their preferences concerning the three types of models discussed here. The neo-Ricardians have a strong preference for the equilibrium model, and in particular a special notion of equilibrium – the long-period equilibrium position. The multiplier mechanism and the adjustment mechanism between saving and investment through changes in income is, in their view, the central contribution of the *General Theory*.[14] The Post Keynesians, on the other hand, emphasize the role of expectations (both short and long) and money.[15] Throughout the book, it shall become clear that whereas the key contributions of the Post Keynesians are to be found in the market-period and historical models, the neo-Ricardian approach is closer to the equilibrium model.

NOTES

1. The endogenous variables in Keynes's short-period equilibrium model in the *General Theory* are the levels of price, output and employment. The exogenous data are the quantity of money, the money wage rate, the propensity to consume, the marginal efficiency of capital and the state of liquidity preference.

2. In fact, the Post Keynesians (and the mainstream Keynesians for that matter) also make use of the short-period equilibrium model. However, the main contributions of the Post Keynesians are associated with the market period and historical models. The neo-Ricardians emphasize a particular notion of equilibrium, the long-period equilibrium in which not only the levels of employment, output and income accommodate to changes in investment, but also the size and composition of the capital stock. We shall discuss these points in more detail in chapters 4 and 5.

3. See Amadeo (1989) for a detailed discussion of the arguments put forward in this section. For a different view, see Patinkin (1976, 1982) and Dimand (1988).

4. Short-term expectations, according to the definition given in the *General Theory*, are concerned

   with the price which a manufacturer can expect to get for his 'finished' output at the time when he commits himself to starting the process which will produce it; output being 'finished' . . . when it is ready to be used or to be sold to a second party. (p. 46)

   The expected price in the simple model presented in the text is represented by P^e. (See also Dutt (1987a).) Note that this refers to expectations by the firm and not by the worker as in chapter 2.

5. As usual, Y is the level of output and N is the level of employment.

6. It should be noted that, although Keynes refers to inventory adjustment in the *General Theory*, this is inconsistent with his assumption of perfect competition.

7. Keynes discusses the effect of an unforeseen change in the level of output of the capital goods sector in chapter 10 of the *General Theory*:

   In general . . . we have to take account of the case where the initiative comes from an increase in the output of the capital-goods industries which was not fully foreseen. It is obvious that an initiative of this description only produces its full effect on employment over a period of time. (JMK, VII, p. 122)

8. The multiplier mechanism refers to the effects of an exogenous change in aggregate demand, that is going from one equilibrium to another. The analysis here examines the dynamic path through which such a movement occurs.

9. In their interpretations of this passage, Kregel (1976, p. 212) and Eatwell (in Eatwell and Milgate, 1983, p. 126) misleadingly extend the idea of omission of expectations to long-term expectations.

10. In this chapter Keynes is quite clear about the independent and dependent variables in his short-period equilibrium model. The following passage summarizes the model:

> [W]e can . . . regard our ultimate independent variables as consisting of (1) the three fundamental psychological factors, namely, the psychological propensity to consume, the psychological attitude to liquidity and the psychological expectation of future yield from capital-assets, (2) the wage-unit as determined by the bargains reached between employers and employed, and (3) the quantity of money . . . [T]hese variables determine the national income . . . and the quantity of employment. (JMK, VII, p. 247)

11. Keynes examines the role of long-period expectations and uncertainty in chapters XII and XXIV of the *General Theory*; and the effect of changes in money wages in chapter XIX.

12. Thus, after describing the causal relation between the independent and dependent variables in the short-period equilibrium model, Keynes notes that

> an increment . . . of employment is liable . . . to raise . . . the schedule of liquidity preference; there being three ways in which it will tend to increase the demand for money, inasmuch as the value of output will rise when employment increases even if the wage-unit and prices . . . are unchanged, but, in addition, the wage-unit itself will tend to rise as employment improves, and the increase in output will be accompanied by a rise in prices (in terms of the wage-unit) owing to increasing cost in the short-period.
> Thus the position of equilibrium will be influenced by these repercussions . . . (JMK, VII, pp. 248–9)

13. Keynes's argument runs as follows:

> Since there is imperfect mobility of labour, and wages do not tend to an exact equality of net advantage in different occupations, any individual or group of individuals, who consent to a reduction of money-wages relatively to others, will suffer a *relative* reduction in real wages, which is a sufficient justification for them to resist it. (JMK, VII, p. 14)

14. In Garegnani's words, Keynes's primary concern 'was to establish a single basic proposition, namely, that is the levels of incomes which insure equality between saving and investment' (1976, p. 141).

15. According to Shackle, Keynes 'declares unequivocally that expec-

tations do not rest on anything solid, determinable, demonstrable . . .' (Shackle, cited by Coddington, 1983, p. 62). 'Investment is an *irrational* activity, or a non-rational one . . . This is the message of the *General Theory*' (1967, p. 130).

4. The Neo-Ricardian Keynesians

INTRODUCTION

A group of 'Cambridge economists', with Garegnani, Bharadwaj, Eatwell and Milgate as its most notable members,[1] has been working on a research programme which has Keynes and Sraffa as its primary intellectual sources. It has put forward an interpretation of Keynes's *General Theory* based on the classical 'long period method', and has been studying the adequacy of Sraffa's prices of production system as an alternative theory of value to Keynes's usage of the marginalist theory. The motivation for such a study is twofold: first, to provide Keynes's principle of effective demand with a consistent theory of value; second, to provide a criticism of the marginalist theory of output and employment based, as it is, on the equalization of saving and investment through changes in the rate of interest.[2]

This approach to the economics of Keynes retains the central features of classical political economy, in particular, the separation of the theories of distribution and relative prices on the one hand, and on the other, output, employment, and accumulation.[3] In what follows we shall assess some of the contributions of this approach, which we shall call neo-Ricardian Keynesianism.

This chapter is organized as follows. In the following section we provide an overview of the neo-Ricardian approach to the macroeconomics of Keynes's *General Theory*. Sections entitled, 'The notion of equilibrium', 'The Neo-Ricardian Characterization of the Long-period Position' and 'The Role of Expectations in Neo-Ricardian Analysis' deal with the notions of equilibrium, centres of gravitation, and long-

44

period positions, and the role ascribed to expectations in neo-Ricardian analysis. These sections discuss concepts and definitions which are not very common in the conventional literature on Keynesian economics and macroeconomics, and should be seen as preparatory to the following sections which discuss more substantial issues. The following three sections discuss the theoretical elements of the neo-Ricardian approach. In the section entitled 'The Neo-Ricardian Interpretation of the General Theory', we review the long-period interpretation of the *General Theory* due to Eatwell and Milgate; in 'The Neo-Ricardian Critique of Marginalist Theory' we study the neo-Ricardian critique of the marginalist analysis and, as consequence, Keynes's analysis of the relation between saving and investment; and in 'The Adjustment Process between Saving and Investment and the Monetary aspects of the Neo-Ricardian Approach', we consider the attempt to integrate the theories of interest, profit and prices of production. Finally, we present a critical assessment of the neo-Ricardian approach to Keynesian economics.

AN OVERVIEW OF THE NEO-RICARDIAN APPROACH

In this section we discuss the central elements of the neo-Ricardian approach to the economics of Keynes. The seminal work, indeed the work which contains the basis for the development of this approach, is due to Garegnani (1978-9).[4]

Garegnani starts by distinguishing two groups in that broad group which Keynes referred to in the *General Theory* as classical economists: what he considers to be the 'classical economists' (Smith, Ricardo, Marx, Mill) and the 'marginalist economists' (Wicksell, Marshall, Pigou). The essential element in the distinction of the two groups for the purposes of our analysis is the relation between saving and investment. For the classicals – and this includes Malthus in Garegnani's view – saving and investment were not conceptually different from each other. That is to say, it was assumed that every act of saving necessarily implied an act of investment of the same magnitude:

> [B]oth Malthus and Ricardo always identified decisions to save with decisions to invest: there could therefore be no disagreement between them concerning the existence of factors capable of equilibrating decisions to invest and decisions to save . . . They took as a *fact* that anyone who had saved would have used this saving to employ productive labourers, or would have lent it to others who would have so used it. (Garegnani, 1978–9, p. 26)

Therefore, the divergence between saving and investment, and the mechanism through which the two equilibrate, was not a relevant issue in classical political economy. Garegnani argues therefore that Keynes's attack was directed towards the marginalist theory of the relation between saving and investment, and the corresponding theory of the rate of interest.

It is well known that, after Wicksell, the rate of interest became the central equilibrating variable between saving and investment.[5] According to the neo-Ricardian approach, Keynes's principle of effective demand should be seen as a legitimate substitute for the marginalist analysis of the relation between saving and investment and the rate of interest, which they claim to be potentially inconsistent.[6]

In marginalist analysis, the rate of interest plays the role of the equilibrating variable between saving and investment. It is assumed that saving is a positive function of the rate of interest, and the demand for capital – or, assuming as we shall, that there is only circulating capital, the demand for investment – is negatively related to the rate of interest. The latter relation results from the assumption that there is substitution in production (between capital and labour), decreasing marginal returns and profit maximization. Hence, given the level of employment (say, full employment), if the rate of interest is sensitive to discrepancies between saving and investment, the equilibrium position (when saving equals investment) is associated with the full utilization of capacity. The same argument can be made for the demand and supply for labour, with the real wage playing the role of the adjustment variable. Here again, for a given level of capacity utilization, the equilibrium situation will be characterized by the full employment of labour. Hence, the forces of supply and demand in each market generate a tendency to an equilibrium position in which the factors of production are fully utilized. In principle, as long as investment is negatively related to the rate of interest, and the rate of interest is sensitive to discrepancies between saving and investment, there will be a tendency towards the full employment of labour and capital. The short-run dynamics of the process of adjustment depend crucially on the flexibility of money wages.

Let the volume of saving depend positively on the rate of interest and the level of employment. Suppose an initial situation in which there is unemployment, and therefore, for each level of the rate of interest, the volume of saving is smaller than what it would be in a situation of full employment. Assume next that if money wages start falling, producers expand the level of output and employment due to the increase in profitability. This will shift the saving function to the right (in Figure 4.1), and the system will shift from point A to point B.

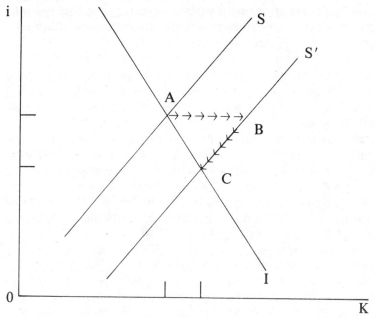

Figure 4.1

If the interest rate is sensitive to a divergence between saving and investment, it will start falling, until the point at which saving and investment are equal again (point C). Suppose that this process of adjustment continues as long as there is unemployment. At the end, both capital and labour will be fully adjusted. What are the conditions for this process, leading to a situation of full employment of the factors of production, to take place? First, money wages must be flexible, that is sensitive to discrepancies between the supply and demand for labour. Second, the rate of interest must be sensitive to discrepancies between saving and investment – that is, it must increase when investment is greater than saving, and vice-versa. Third, the slopes of the saving and investment functions must be such that the system is stable. Given the slope of the saving function, the latter condition implies a restriction on the slope of the investment function.[7]

Based on the results of the so-called 'capital controversy',[8] neo-Ricardians argue that there is no reason to believe that the investment function will always have the appropriate slope in order to satisfy the third condition. In a system with heterogeneous capital goods and multiple techniques of production, the slope of the investment function can change sign as the rate of interest increases. Obviously, this undermines the consistency of the marginalist explanation for the tendency of the system towards a position of full employment and full utilization of capacity.[9]

It is well known that Keynes in the *General Theory* accepted Fisher's notion of marginal efficiency of capital (which maintains a decreasing relation with the stock of capital), and thus assumed a negatively sloped investment demand function. Neo-Ricardians see this assumption to be a throwback to the marginalists, which made possible the rehabilitation of the marginalist analysis in the inter-war period.

As noted in chapter 2, Keynes did not see wage rigidity as the fundamental cause of unemployment. However, if wages are flexible and the investment function is downward sloping, there will be a tendency to full employment unless the interest rate is not sensitive to discrepancies between saving and investment. Indeed, Keynes's theory of liquidity preference isolated the determination of the rate of interest from the forces driving the supply and demand for funds, and instead he argued that the rate of interest regulated the demand and supply for liquidity. This, however, does not prevent the rate of interest from being affected in a process of wage and price deflation: Keynes himself argued that an increase in the real value of outstanding money could have the effect of reducing the interest rate.

The neo-Ricardians see Keynes's theory of the determination of the rate of interest as being incapable of supporting his claim for the possibility of chronic unemployment.[10] The theory is seen as a short-period analysis according to which the speculative demand for money depends on the divergence between the actual and the 'normal' rate of interest – but the latter is not explained by the theory. Instead, the neo-Ricardians think that a more fundamental criticism of the marginalist approach would have to focus on the problems associated with the determinant of the value of capital, and hence the slope of the investment function.

THE NOTION OF EQUILIBRIUM

The neo-Ricardian approach is centred on the notion of long-period (equilibrium) positions of the economic system,[11] that is, positions towards or around which the relevant variables gravitate. Before discussing the specific neo-Ricardian characterization of equilibrium positions, it will be useful to consider an abstract notion of the term, and its relationship to the Marshallian usage of the terms short and long periods. Consider a system composed of a set of data (parameters and independent variables), a set of endogenously determined variables, and a set of functional relations between the variables of the system. To any change in the data, there will correspond a new configuration of the endogenous variables. An equilibrium simply describes this final configuration towards or around which the system gravitates. Equilibrium refers to a position of systemic rest associated with a given set of exogenous variables and the parameters specifying the (expectational, behavioural and technological) functional relations of the system. According to this notion of the term, disequilibrium positions are associated with the transitory path between two positions of rest. They are, so to speak, unstable positions whereas equilibrium positions are stable in the sense that, for a given set of values of thc data variables, once the system reaches the equilibrium configuration there will not be any (combination of) forces capable of driving the system out of that position.[12]

We may refer to the data *cum* functional relations which characterize the system as its 'core'.[13] Feedback effects from the endogenous variables to the data and between the elements of the data may occur but they are not considered explicitly since this would essentially imply the redefinition of the equilibrium. The decision as to which are the exogenous and endogenous variables depends very much on the specific purpose of the analysis. Accordingly, the relevant variables for the characterization of the equilibrium position will depend on the choice of the determined and determinant variables.[14] There are different reasons why a variable should be part of the data rather than an endogenous variable. The three main ones are the following. First, the variable in question may depend more on factors alien to the system than on the dynamics of the system. This is usually the case with variables determined by historical and institutional factors in classical political economy (the real wage being the best example here), and the case of variables or relations affected by psychological factors such as preferences in neo-classical economics. Second, the variable in question may maintain multiple and highly unsystematic functional relations with one or more of the variables of the system thus weakening the definiteness of the results.[15] The third reason is associated with the span of historical time underlying the analysis: chronological considerations resulting from the purpose of the analysis influence the logical structure of the system. Analyses associated with a short time horizon generally will have a greater number of givens than analyses in which the underlying time span is longer. The longer the period the greater the flexibility of the system and, therefore, in principle, the greater the number of endogenous variables. These considerations lead us to Marshall's notions of short and long periods.

Marshall (1890) made use of the terms short and long periods in a very specific fashion. In the short periods, he writes

[t]he supply of specialized skill and ability, of suitable machinery and other material capital, and of the appropriate industrial organization has not time to be fully adapted to demand . . . In long periods on the other hand all investments of capital and effort in providing the material, plant and organization of a business . . . have time to be adjusted to the incomes which are expected to be earned by them . . . (Marshall, 1890, p. 313)

Both the short and long periods may correspond to equilibrium positions, and when they do correspond, the price levels associated with each of these positions will be referred to as 'normal prices':

In each [period], price is governed by the relations between demand and supply . . . As regards normal prices, when the term Normal is taken to relate to short periods . . . supply means broadly what can be produced for the price in question with the existing stock of plant . . . [W]hen the term Normal is to refer to long periods . . . supply means what can be produced by plant, which itself can be remuneratively produced and applied within the given price . . . (Marshall, 1890, pp. 314–15)

Thus the short period may be characterized by a given size and composition of the productive capacity; only the utilization of capacity and the employment of the variable inputs adjust to demand. In the long period both the sectoral structure and size of the stock of capital (capacity itself) adjust to changes in demand.

A combination of the notions of equilibrium and disequilibrium, and the Marshallian specific usage of the terms short and long periods gives rise to Table 4.1.

In the Marshallian short period, disequilibrium positions are associated with the adjustment of capacity utilization and employment. The equilibrium position, in turn, corresponds to the final configuration of employment and utilization. Once capacity itself starts adjusting to demand (the Marshallian long period) the analysis is supposed to discuss the process according to which the stock of capital changes (across a series

Table 4.1 Short- and long-period equilibrium and disequilibrium positions

Positions Marshallian notions of	disequilibrium	equilibrium
short period	adjustment variables: employment and utilization	final configuration of employment and utilization
long period	adjustment variables: structure and size of capacity	final configuration of the structure and size of capacity (normal capacity utilization)

of disequilibrium positions), and the determination of the final configuration of the sectoral structure and size of the stock of capital. In equilibrium firms are assumed to operate at the normal or desired degree of utilization.

It should be noted that Keynes, *en route* to the *General Theory*, considered three alternative notions of equilibrium positions (long-period positions in Keynes's terminology) – not mutually exclusive – which are quite in accordance with the definitions presented here. He writes that:

> there are three suggestions conveyed by the term [long-period], which are differently dominant on different occasions of its use. The first suggestion conveyed by the term 'long period' is that it relates to a position towards which forces spring up to influence the short-period position whenever the latter has diverged from it. The second suggestion conveyed is that the long-period position differs from the short-period positions in being a stable position capable *cet. par.* of being sustained, whilst short-period positions are *cet. par.* unstable and cannot be sustained. The third suggestion is that the long-period position is, in some sense, an optimum or ideal position from the point of view of production. (JMK, XXIX, p. 54)

The first two suggestions are quite in accordance with the notion of equilibrium positions discussed above. The first suggestion refers to the relation between short- and long-period positions whereas the second is associated with the stability of both positions. The third one refers to the adjustment of the structure of production to the conditions of demand, and, therefore, maintains close relation with Marshall's dichotomy. Keynes does not differentiate, however, between the Marshallian short and long periods. It is significant that in relation to the third suggestion Keynes notes that 'there is no reason to suppose that positions of long-period equilibrium have an inherent tendency or likelihood to be positions of optimum output' (JMK, XXIX, p. 55). This could be interpreted as meaning that in neither instances of the equilibrium position (long or short) capacity utilization necessarily matches the normal or desired degree.

THE NEO-RICARDIAN CHARACTERIZATION OF THE LONG-PERIOD POSITION

We may now turn to the neo-Ricardian characterization of the equilibrium (or, in the neo-Ricardian terminology, long-period) position. According to this approach

[a] capitalist economy is said to exhibit long-period characteristics (to be 'in' a long-period position) if, when the price of each commodity is uniform throughout the system, a *general* (uniform) rate of profit on the supply-price of capital associated with the dominant . . . technique obtains. (Milgate, 1982, p. 12)

Furthermore, 'the uniformity of the rate of profit (. . .) requires that the scale and composition of output and the size and composition of capacity are adjusted one to the other' (Eatwell, 1983, p. 271). It is obvious from the second condition that the equilibrium position corresponds to the usage of the term associated with the Marshallian long period since the size and structure of capacity are supposed to be compatible with the scale and composition of output or demand. Therefore, this characterization is not consistent with situations in which capacity does not correspond to its normal level as suggested by Keynes in the passage quoted above.[16]

The mechanism through which the system gravitates around (or converges toward) the equilibrium position as characterized by a uniform rate of profit is the 'operation of free competition in a capitalist economy [which] induces capitalists to seek the most profitable employment of their stock' (Milgate, 1982, p. 24).[17] The notion of gravitation around the equilibrium position implies that the latter corresponds to an average position (or a steady state) around which the economy actually oscillates. Deviations of market prices (and actual output for that matter) from the normal prices (and output) levels may result from temporary or non-persistent phenomena such as expectational errors. The averaging out over time of these deviations which are associated with 'incongruities between existing plant and demand for products', i.e., deviations from the normal level of capacity utilization, 'is one and the same thing as gravitation around a uniform, "normal" rate of profits calculated on the supply price of the means of production' (Garegnani, 1979, p. 76).[18]

The notion of 'long-period position' plays a central part in neo-Ricardian economics. However, the emphasis on the notion of equilibrium does not have any implication for the actual or historical movement of the economy as envisaged by neo-Ricardians. Indeed, the notion of a 'central' or 'natural' position plays the part of an 'organizing concept', and does not have any descriptive connotation. Bharadwaj, referring to a passage by Robertson which we quote below, notes that 'the notion of equilibrium [does not] imply that the economy [will] achieve equilibrium. However, that equilibrium may never be achieved in practice [is] not considered sufficient to deny the tendency towards it' (1985, p. 23). The passage by Robertson makes these points quite clear:

['T]ends in the long run to equal' does not mean equals . . . We must not think of the long run value of a thing as something which will be attained after so many months or years and then stay put. It is more nearly legitimate to think of it as a norm around which actual values oscillate . . . yet even that conception though helpful may be too clearcut for application to a changing world. It may be that in such a world, long run equilibrium is never attained. It is the state of affairs which could be attained if all the forces at work had time to work themselves out. (in Robertson, 1957, vol. I, pp. 6–8; quoted by Bharadwaj, 1985, p. 23)

The long-period position is thought of as an average situation around which the system oscillates. Conventionally, this average position is associated with the notions of 'steady state' or 'balanced path' of the system. However, some neo-Ricardians think that the 'identification of long-period analysis with steady state appears to be unduly restrictive, given the highly artificial features of steady states' (Committeri, 1986, p. 169). Amongst these restrictions, it is argued that in steady state models, mistaken expectations and divergences between desired and actual levels of output and prices are usually neglected. It is our view that there are no great differences between steady state and centres of gravitation models, and in what follows we compare the two varieties of models.

The concept of steady state has two different dimensions. The more general one refers to an equilibrium position characterized by the equilibrium configuration of the endogenous variables associated with a given set of data variables. The second dimension is associated with the configuration of the relevant variables towards which the system converges or around which the system gravitates. The process of adjustment is emphasized in the second dimension, and a set of conditions concerning the stability of the process must be satisfied. Expectations play an important part in the stability of the process of adjustment, and in fact, their definitions are closely associated with the part they play.

Expectations are affected by two sets of factors. First, past and current events affect the 'short-period' expectations. Agents take these events as an approximation for what is to come in the immediate future. The other set of factors which determine the 'long-period' expectations is composed of new information, the institutional setting in which decisions are taken and the psychology of decision makers. In steady state analysis, the components of the first set of factors are allowed to change during adjustment processes whereas the determinants of the second set of factors are assumed to be frozen. Changes in the first group of factors affect the system between two positions of equilibrium, but not the equilibrium position itself. Changes in the second group of factors affect the equilibrium position. This construction has restrictive features but it yields very definite results in the study of the adjustment process (and stability analysis) and the comparison between equilibria.

The steady state construction plays the same role as the neo-Ricardian notion of centre of gravitation. In the latter, according to Ciccone (1986, p. 23), 'there is . . . room for the fluctuations in quantities and prices and disappointment of expectations that occur in reality'. These characteristics, it should be noted, are not incompatible with steady state analysis. In comparing the notions of centres of gravitation and steady states, it is not quite clear why the assumptions surrounding the latter should be more restrictive than those associated with the former. Stability conditions, the particular mechanisms which permeate the functioning of 'competition' between capitals and the formation of expectations are all issues faced in steady state models, and which should also be faced in centres of gravitation models. The differences between the two types of models should not be over emphasized because they are not really fundamental. Steady state models can be seen as a particular case of centres of gravitation models in which the functional relations of the system (including expectational relations) are explicitly specified. This particular characteristic of these models allow them to yield definite configurations for the dependent variables associated with a given set of data variables. The results of centres of gravitation models may be more general, but they clearly tend to be less conclusive.[19]

In the previous section reference was made to the notion of the 'core' of a system by which we meant the set of data and endogenous variables and the set of functional relations between those same variables. The core of the neo-Ricardian system is composed of three sets of *data* variables – the wage rate (or the uniform rate of profit), the methods of production, and the size and composition of output. The endogenous variables are the relative prices and the rate of profit (or wage rate measured in terms of the price of one of the reproducible commodities).[20] The functional relations are a set of price equations according to which prices are determined by the costs of production and the rate of profit on capital advanced.

Feedback effects can be studied, and indeed,

the treatment of the real wage, the social product and the technical conditions of production as independent variables in the 'core' in no way entail[s] denying the existence of influences of any single one of these three sets of variables over the remaining two. (Garegnani, 1984, p.296)

The reason for treating them as independent variables is that the multiplicity of influences of, say, a change in the real wage on the level of output, the methods of production and relative prices may render the results of the analysis much less definite.[21] Neo-Ricardians see the 'separation' of the theories of prices and output or the 'openness' of the classical system of prices concerning alternative theories of output determination as an advantage of the model. The separation of the theories of prices and output and accumulation

opens the possibilities of introducing a wider range of determinants and the real dynamics of the process of change; precisely because thereby the more complex, historical institutional and social specificities that influence changes, particularly in distribution, technology of production, and investment could be introduced without being constrained to the purely exchange-based sphere of price formation. (Bharadwaj, 1985, p. 28)

A consistent theoretical construction requires a clear distinction between givens and endogenous variables, and that is precisely what the openness of the neo-Ricardian model implies. However, interactive effects between data variables and endogenous variables must be considered if and when closures are to be appended to the classical or neo-Ricardian system. One such closure would be Keynes's theory of output as proposed by the neo-Ricardians themselves.[22] Potential effects to be considered would be the influence of distribution on aggregate demand and output, the influence of changes in the scale of output on the methods of production and, therefore, on relative prices. Neo-Ricardians have been quite timid in exploring alternative closures, and have for that reason been accused of taking too many things as 'givens'.[23] Indeed, it could be argued that neo-Ricardians have systematically neglected the out-of-core elements of the theory, and that, in particular, aggregate demand aspects (which must be considered in a general analysis of the capitalist economy) such as the determinants of investment demand, the relation between the distribution of income and the level of consumption demand, and wealth effects have all been practically ignored. By the same token, the relations between nominal variables (such as the money supply and the money wage rate) and real variables (say, relative prices and output), and the short-period dynamics involving these relations, have not received enough attention from neo-Ricardians.[24]

THE ROLE OF EXPECTATIONS IN NEO-RICARDIAN ANALYSIS

Some critics of the neo-Ricardian approach – most notably Joan Robinson and the Post Keynesians – have pointed out a certain discrepancy between the notion of equilibrium and the role of expectations and uncertainty. Joan Robinson's view is that '[a]s soon as the uncertainty of the expectations that guide economic behaviour is admitted, equilibrium drops out of the argument and history takes its place' (1974, p.48). As for the specific role of expectations in equilibrium analysis she argues that 'long-period balance could be continuously maintained only on a steady growth path where confident expectations about the future can be maintained, continuously fulfilled and so renewed' (1978, p. 214). Therefore the existence of uncertainty and expectations threatens the relevance of equilibrium analysis and, in particular, comparative statics analysis which omits the role of expectations whenever the system deviates from the equilibrium position.

It is true that the neo-Ricardians have neglected almost altogether the role of expectations and uncertainty, and that this imposes serious limits on the scope of their analysis, especially the short-run analysis. In general, neo-Ricardians assume that short-run analysis should not be given too much importance, or in other words that adjustment processes and expectations are relatively irrelevant, and that only changes in the objective factors should be taken into account to explain the long-period position of the system. But, clearly enough, there are periods of great uncertainty in which expectations change quite rapidly and the behaviour of the economic agents change accordingly. The more these changes affect the behaviour of the agents, and more importantly, the conventions and institutions which permeate the economic and social life, the greater becomes the necessity to consider them in long-period analysis. Otherwise, it seems that important changes in the economic environment – due to changes in objective factors and repercussions through the formation of expectations – could not find an explanation in the theory.

It seems, therefore, that the Post Keynesian emphasis on the role of uncertainty and expectations does provide some important elements for the study of capitalist economies. However, there are two problematic aspects associated with the use of expectations in economic theory which must be considered. First, the formation of expectations, especially under uncertainty, is very hard to generalize in a way which could become really useful in economic analysis. Second, because we know so little about the way expectations are formed, we tend to follow one of two radical (and simplistic) routes:

i. to assume that agents know exactly the way the system works, and therefore can only have their expectations falsified when stochastic events occur – the rational expectations hypothesis in its strongest version;

ii. or to render uncertainty and the volatility of expectations such an important role, that the notions of equilibrium and stability become virtually irrelevant – the radical Post Keynesian view.

The notions of equilibrium and disequilibrium (and steady state path) discussed in the previous paragraphs are powerful instruments of analysis. Given alternative assumptions about what are the data and what the endogenous variables, and the functional relations between them, the equilibrium method has the quite desirable characteristic of providing definite results. Furthermore, the method is not entirely incompatible with disequilibrium analysis which may arise, *inter alia*, from expectational errors. As noted in chapter 3, the notion of equilibrium is only the first step to understanding the systematic relations between a set of variables. Institutional factors and the caveats resulting from the irreversibility of time (and particularly expectations) may then be introduced as factors affecting the determination of the data variables and the parameters of the functional relations to make the results more relevant.

The neo-Ricardian position concerning the role of expectations is not that they should not be taken into account but that they ought not be given such a disturbing role as to render the analysis devoid of any definite result (see Garegnani, 1976, p. 140). Expectations should instead play the role of the 'accidental (non-persistent) forces' which make the actual path of the system (associated with the 'market prices' and actual utilization of capacity) deviate from the normal position.[25] Expectations are supposed to be satisfied in equilibrium through the 'averaging out process' of deviations from the norm, a result which is implied in the notion that expectations cannot be persistently falsified.

THE NEO-RICARDIAN INTERPRETATION OF THE GENERAL THEORY

In face of this discussion where does Keynes's *General Theory* lie in terms of methods of analysis? There seems to be no doubt that, unlike the *Treatise* in which Keynes concentrates on deviations from a norm, the objective of the *General Theory* is to argue for the possibility of a norm characterized by involuntary unemployment. From our point of view, neo-Ricardians have correctly emphasized the importance of the equilibrium model in the *General Theory*.[26]

There is no fundamental difference amongst most Keynesians about the nature of the equilibrium position in the *General Theory*.[27] The disagreement starts with Eatwell and Milgate's most controversial claim that the *General Theory* is cast in a 'long-period' analysis. What does this mean? Does it mean equilibrium analysis or does the term long-period analysis mean something more than this? This seems to be the relevant question if we want to understand the controversy over the long-period interpretation of Keynes's *General Theory*.[28]

According to Joan Robinson, '[t]he *General Theory* is set in a strictly "short period" situation . . . Keynes hardly ever peered over the edge of the short period to see the effect of investment in making addition to the stock of productive equipment' (1978, pp. 211–12). Critics of Eatwell and Milgate's interpretation follow Joan Robinson's view. They argue that changes in the scale and composition of the stock of capital are not considered by Keynes in the *General Theory* and that, indeed, the model developed in the book is based on Marshall's notion of short-period equilibrium.[29] Critics also argue that Keynes's analysis focuses on the determination of the levels of capacity utilization rather than the adjustment of capacity to changes in demand. Accordingly, the object of analysis of the *General Theory* is the 'theory of employment' rather than the 'theory of accumulation'. Garegnani, himself a prominent neo-Ricardian, disagrees with Eatwell and Milgate, and argues that

it should be clear that Keynes is concerned with a short-period analysis of aggregate output (the determination of capacity utilization) and that a long-period analysis of aggregate output, i.e, an analysis of the reciprocal adaptation of aggregate supply and aggregate demand is one and the same thing as a theory of accumulation. This is absent in Keynes . . . (Eatwell and Milgate, 1983, Preface)

From the point of view of the adjustment of the size of capacity to the scale of output, therefore, the critics' main point is that the *General Theory* refers to the Marshallian short period.

Eatwell and Milgate, however, disagree with the idea that Keynes's *General Theory* should be identified with the Marshallian short period. The root of the controversy involving their interpretation is the extent to which capacity adjusts to demand in Keynes's analysis. A long-period analysis must consider changes in the level and composition of the stock of capital. Given a change in autonomous demand and output, if the size and composition of capacity do not change, only the degree of capacity utilization will adjust. In this case, only by coincidence, the composition of the stock of capital would be compatible with the composition of demand, and the rate of profit would be uniform across sectors. It is also obvious that in this case the size of the stock of capital would not be compatible with the volume of output and, therefore, that firms would not be operating at the normal or desired level of utilization. This only means that, in principle, none of the characteristics of a long-period position would hold after the change in demand. Thus, capacity must adjust for the conditions of 'normality' to hold.

What is then the interpretation of Eatwell and Milgate of Keynes's assumption of givenness of 'the existing quality and quantity of available equipment'? Although they do not spell it out in this way, the interpretation seems to be that capacity is given *in* the long period rather than *during* the process of adjustment; whereas the conventional interpretation is that capacity is given during the workings of the multiplier mechanism, that is, over the adjustment process. According to Milgate,

[a]n interpretation of Keynes more in line with his own theory and less likely to lead to errors of interpretation would therefore appear to hinge on the recognition that it was designed not to limit the analysis to a Marshallian short-period but rather to allow the analysis to proceed without the need to consider the 'results of far reaching social changes or . . . the slow effects of secular progress' (JMK, VII, p. 109) due to changes in technology, accumulation and the like. (Milgate, 1984, p. 90)

It seems clear from this passage that Eatwell and Milgate believe that a more general and fruitful interpretation of Keynes's assumption about the givenness of the stock of capital is the one according to which the analysis refers to Marshall's 'stationary state' rather than Marshall's 'short-period'. Indeed, their view is that a general theory of employment should not be confined to the short period, but rather to the long period. In the long period, capacity and demand are balanced in size and composition but, as noted by Eatwell and Milgate, there is no guarantee that the available labour force will be fully employed. In short, the normal (or full) utilization of capacity does not imply the full employment of labour. In

Milgate's words, 'capacity utilization will become "full" in the face of [the adjustment of capacity to output] but unemployment will persist' (1984, p. 90) This is what the proponents of the long-period version of Keynes's principle of effective demand consider to be the appropriate conception of structural or chronic unemployment.

It is admitted that Keynes 'did not devote his efforts [in the *General Theory*] to the construction of an explicitly long-period theory' (Eatwell, 1983, p. 273). However, Keynes does extend his principle of effective demand to long-period analysis in his chapter 16, and the model there developed is very similar to the one put forward by Eatwell and Milgate. The analysis starts from a Marshallian stationary state situation in which the marginal efficiency of capital is equal to the rate of interest, implying that there is not any net investment taking place. Full employment is also assumed as part of the initial conditions. What is the effect of a positive net propensity to save in this situation? According to Keynes, 'entrepreneurs will necessarily make losses if they continue to offer employment of a scale which utilizes the whole of the existing stock of capital' (JMK, VII, p. 217). In fact, if the net propensity to save is positive, then the aggregate level of net saving compatible with the full employment of labour will be positive and greater than net investment.

Therefore, for a given level of net propensity to consume, there is only one level of employment (necessarily smaller than full employment) for which saving and investment will be equal. According to Keynes, 'for a society such as we have supposed, the position of equilibrium . . . will be one in which employment is low enough and the standard of life sufficiently miserable to bring [net] saving to zero' (JMK, VII, p. 217). As the level of output falls, the stock of capital will gradually adjust and, in fact, it will be reduced to a point in which 'the equilibrium stock of capital . . . will . . . be smaller than would correspond to full employment of the available labour' (JMK, VII, p. 218). Thus, in Keynes's long-period exercise, developed in the *General Theory*, unemployment results from the incompatibility between the propensity to consume and the full employment level of demand, given the rate of interest and the state of long-period expectations. The new stationary equilibrium in this model will be characterized by the normal utilization of capacity but not by the full employment of the available labour force.

It can be argued that Keynes's *General Theory's* central object of analysis is the Marshallian short period – and indeed, from our perspective, this is the correct interpretation[30] – but it seems that Eatwell and Milgate can legitimately claim that in the book Keynes extended his main model to long-period situations.[31] There are three aspects of this interpretation which deserve special attention. First, we should distinguish an interpretation of the *General Theory* which claims that Keynes's main focus in the book was the long-period position of the economic system (which is Eatwell and Milgate's view) from the idea that the model developed in the book could be extended to entertain long-period situations. It is difficult to agree with the first idea but we certainly agree with the second.

Second, this approach does not consider short-period adjustment processes, and therefore neglects the stability conditions of the system. In particular, it is worth noting that in the short period, the rates of profits of the various sectors will not be in line, and that the 'competition between capitals' will have worked as a mechanism to take the system back to a long-period equilibrium position. In this process, expectations on the part of entrepreneurs will be an important factor, and it is quite clear that they will affect, if not the equilibrium position, the path of the system. The analysis of these phenomena is seldomly considered by neo-Ricardians.

The third point to be considered is the extent to which neo-Ricardians analyse the reciprocal process of adjustment of changes in output and capacity. In particular, what determines the level of investment and what is the relationship between changes in aggregate demand and investment demand? If the neo-Ricardian or classical system is in fact open to alternative closures concerning the determinants of output and investment, why not examine the implications of the alternative closures? Indeed, it is not quite clear that independently from the closure assumed, the equilibrium position will be characterized by the existence of unemployed labour. If the adjustment process assumes a Kaleckian (or Keynesian) investment function, it seems obvious that full employment will not be necessarily a characteristic of the long-period position.[32] However, if neo-classical assumptions are made, there is no good reason to suppose that the system will not converge to a full employment position. Neo-Ricardians will always claim that the neo-classical model lacks consistency (something that we shall examine presently) but at least in principle it is legitimate to argue that, if a 'well behaved' neo-classical system were assumed, the model would converge to a full employment position. In sum, as noted already, the problem is that neo-Ricardians seldom make explicit the closure being assumed.

THE NEO-RICARDIAN CRITIQUE OF MARGINALIST THEORY

We may now consider the neo-Ricardian contribution to economic theory as such. The careful reconstruction of the classical system by Sraffa (1960) – from which the neo-Ricardian approach to the economics of Keynes was developed – has the great merit of revealing some problems associated with the marginalist theory of value and distribution based on aggregate production functions. It can be shown that in a system with more than one reproducible commodity the value of any given vector of physical quantities is not independent from the distribution of income between wages and profits. As a result, it can also be shown that the value of any given physical stock of capital does not maintain a monotonic (inverse) relation with the rate of profit as contended by the marginalist theory.[33] This result is in turn used to show that the curve representing the demand for capital (or investment) does not maintain necessarily a monotonic relation with the rate of interest.

Neo-Ricardians have extended these results to a critique of the marginalist theory of output and employment. In their view, Keynes's analysis in the *General Theory* retained some orthodox or marginalist elements which, on the one hand, did not allow him to develop a negative critique of the orthodox theory (in the sense of showing its inconsistencies), and on the other hand, left open the road for a return of the marginalist theory now incorporating some of Keynes's positive contributions.[34] The neo-Ricardian critique of the marginalist theory of output and employment is due essentially to Garegnani (1978-9).[35] In what follows we present a summary of the arguments leading to the neo-Ricardian critique of marginal analysis, including Keynes's own use of marginal analysis in the *General Theory*.

We start with a stylized neo-classical model of an economy which employs labour and an homogeneous commodity (corn-capital) to produce this same commodity (corn).[36] We assume continuous substitution between labour and capital, decreasing marginal returns and profit maximization. If we assume that corn-capital cannot be carried from one period of production to the next, then there will be no difference between capital and gross investment in this economy, and hence there will be no difference either between the demand for capital and the demand for investment.

If we fix the amount of labour in use (say at full employment), then the marginal product of corn-capital will be a decreasing function of the rate of profit due to the assumptions of profit maximization and decreasing marginal returns. Refer to Figure 4.2. The curve representing the marginal product of capital (MP_c) can be seen as the demand function for capital (or investment); it relates the optimum amount of capital to be used by producers to each level of the rate of profit.

In marginalist analysis, if the system is in equilibrium, the rate of interest should be equal to the rate of profit. Hence, we can use the terms 'rate of interest' and 'rate of profits' interchangeably. We assume that saving is a positive function of the rate of interest and the level of employment (curve S in Figure 4.2). There is a rate of profit ($r = r^*$) for which the supply and demand for corn-capital are equal. If there is excess demand of capital, that is when $r < r^*$, investors will be prepared to pay a higher rate of interest to savers, and the rate on interest will tend to increase until the point in which

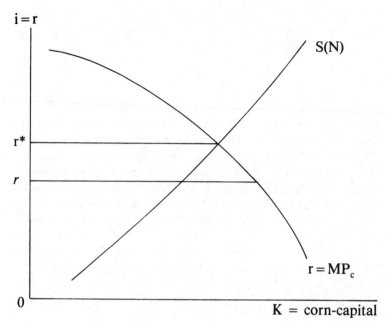

Figure 4.2

demand and supply match. The equilibrium position is characterized by the full utilization of the corn supplied, given the level of employment.

In sum, in this simple model,

i. the demand curve for corn-capital (investment) is a decreasing function of the rate of interest; hence, the lower the rate of interest the greater the *volume* of corn-capital demanded;
ii. the rate of interest equilibrates saving and investment;
iii. for a given level of employment, there is full utilization of the corn-capital supplied (at the equilibrium rate of interest); and for a given volume of capital in use, there is full employment of the labour supplied.

We may now move on to a second model in which there are two commodities and only one technique of production available to producers (in other words, fixed coefficients of production). In this simple two-sector example, the price equations can be written as follows:

$$1 = wb_1 + R(a_{11} + a_{21}p) \tag{4.1}$$

$$p = wb_2 + R(a_{12} + a_{22}p) \tag{4.2}$$

where: commodity 1 is the numeraire, a_{ij} represents the amount of commodity i required to produce 1 unit of commodity j, w is the real wage measured in terms of commodity 1, $R = (1 + r)$ is the uniform gross rate of profit, b_i is the labour input in the production of commodity i, and p is the relative price of commodity 2 in relation to commodity 1, that is, $p = p_2/p_1$.[37] The value of capital in this model is given by:

$$K = p' AX \tag{4.3}$$

where $p' = [1, p]$, $X' = [X_1, X_2]$, the vector of gross output levels and $A = [a_{ij}]$ the input-output matrix. The relative price can be written as a function of the rate of profit:

$$p = [b_2 + R(a_{12}b_1 + a_{11}b_2)]/[b_1 + R(a_{21}b_2 + a_{22}b_1)]$$

The relation between the relative price and the rate of profit is given by the following expression:

$$dp/dR =$$

$$[b_1(a_{12}b_1 - a_{11}b_2) - b_2(a_{21}b_2 - a_{21}b_2)]/\{b_1 + R[a_{21}b_2 - a_{22}b_1]\}^2$$

These expressions imply simply that, in general, the relative price will depend on the rate of profit. Let us now fix the level of employment at the full employment level ($N = N_f$) just as in the simple case with a homogeneous commodity and continuous substitution. This assumption implies that the vector $X = X_f$ must be such that

$$b'X_f = N_f$$

where b is the column vector of labour inputs. Note that the value of capital can now be written as:

$$K(R) = p'(R) AX_f$$

that is, the value of capital, *given* a vector X_f and matrix A, is a function of the rate of profit.

This simple case can be generalized to consider a system with n reproducible commodities in which, in principle, any commodity can either be consumed or used as an input in the production of any other commodity in the system. In this case the price system would be written as follows:

$$1 = b_1 w + R (a_{11} + a_{21}p_2 + \ldots + a_{n1}p_n)$$
$$p_2 = b_2 w + R (a_{12} + a_{22}p_2 + \ldots + a_{n2}p_n)$$

$$\ldots \quad \ldots \quad \ldots \quad \ldots \quad \ldots \quad \ldots \quad \ldots \quad \ldots \quad \ldots \quad \ldots$$
$$\ldots \quad \ldots \quad \ldots \quad \ldots \quad \ldots \quad \ldots \quad \ldots \quad \ldots \quad \ldots \quad \ldots \quad (4.4)$$

$$p_n = b_n w + R (a_{1n} + a_{2n}p_2 + \ldots + + a_{nn}p_n)$$

Th system can be written in matrix notation as follows:

$$p' = R p'A + b' w \qquad (4.5)$$

where the real wage is evaluated in terms of commodity 1. The relation between the real wage, the rate of profit and the relative prices is given by the expression:

$$p' = b' [I - RA]^{-1} w \qquad (4.6)$$

where I is the identity matrix. If the rate of profit is given exogenously, the real wage and the n–1 relative prices will be determined endogenously.[38] In order to derive the relation between the rate of profit and the wage rate, we post-multiply equation 4.6 by the first unit vector $e_1 = (1, 0, \ldots,)$:[39]

$$1 = b' [I - RA]^{-1} e_1 w \qquad (4.7)$$

In general, the relation between the real wage and the rate of profit is obviously not linear. The value of capital in the general case is also given by expression 4.3:

$$K(R) = \mathbf{p}'(R)\mathbf{AX} \qquad (4.8)$$

In the case of an n–commodity system, just as in the simple bi-sectoral model, relative prices are not independent of the rate of profit (or more generally, the distribution of income), and the relation between the real wage and the rate of profit (as depicted in Figure 4.3) is not linear.[40] Also, because relative

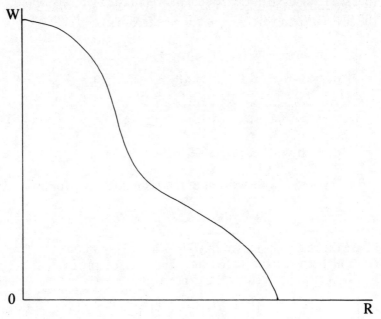

Figure 4.3

prices depend on the distribution of income, the value of capital (K) does not maintain a monotonic relation with the rate of profit.

Note that in both the simple two-sector case and the general n–commodity case, the physical volume and composition of capital ($\mathbf{AX}_f$) do not change with a change in the rate of profit. We now turn to a last case in which we combine the effect of changes in the rate of profit on relative prices (as in the two cases just considered) and the effect on the physical volume and composition of capital.

Consider an economy with various capital goods and more than one technique of production available to producers. It will be assumed that producers will choose the most profitable technique given the rate of profit. In this case, it can be shown that there will be as many <w, r> frontiers (as the one depicted in Figure 4.3) as there are techniques of production. Assuming that producers minimize costs, it can also be shown that the relevant frontier for each level of the real wage will be the one which yields the highest profit rate.[41] In Figure 4.4a,

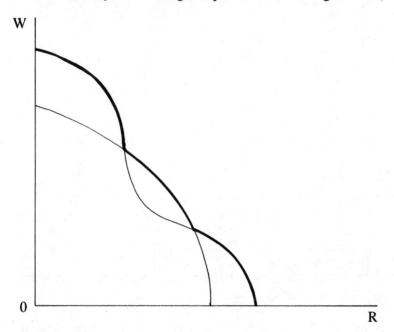

Figure 4.4a

the bold line represents the relevant frontier.

It should be noted that in the present case both relative prices and the physical volume and composition of the stock of capital will change as the rate of profit changes. The effect over the physical stock of capital results from the change in the technique of production. As the rate of profit increases, producers will choose different techniques, each one with a

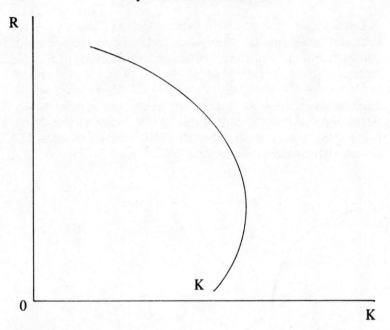

Figure 4.4b

different physical capital profile. In general, the same technique will be chosen for different segments of the rate of
profit, implying that the system will shift back and forth from
techniques with greater physical capital content to techniques
with a lower capital content.

Hence, in a system with heterogeneous capital goods and
alternative techniques, there will be changes in both relative
prices and physical capital as the rate of profit changes. It is
important to note that the changes in the physical stock of
capital in the present case do not correspond to the changes
generally derived from neo-classical models. Based on the
assumptions of a homogeneous commodity and continuous
substitution between labour and capital (just as in the very
first model examined above), neo-classical models predict that
the capital content will necessarily increase as the rate of profit
falls. However, as Garegnani (1978–9, p. 40) notes, in the
heterogeneous commodity case, when the relative price effect
and the physical capital effect are taken into account,

it seems that little or nothing of general validity can be said concerning the form of the relationship between the value of physical capital and the rate of interest. If we represent the relationship on a diagram, with the rate of interest on the vertical axis, the curve may just as well slope up to the right as down to the right, and it may alternate such slopes any number of times.

Figure 4b depicts one possible relation between the value of capital and the rate of profit. Neo-Ricardians interpret this curve as a legitimate analog in a heterogeneous commodity case of the capital or investment demand curve in the single-commodity model.[42] Thus, they compare the relation between saving and investment in the neo-classical version (homogeneous commodity and variable proportions) with the case just examined (heterogeneous commodities and alternative techniques).

Again, as in the case of the homogeneous commodity model, let saving depend positively on the level of employment and the rate of interest. Also, let the saving function and the stock of capital correspond to the full employment of labour, $S(N_f)$ and $D(N_f)$, respectively. Two alternative combinations of investment demand and supply of capital functions are depicted in Figures 4.5a and 4.5b.

In Figure 4.5a equilibrium *cum* full employment of labour exists but it is obviously unstable. A marginal deviation from equilibrium would lead the system to one of the extremes of the distribution *spectrum*. Garegnani (1978–9, p. 73) observes that if the capital demand curve was to be like the one depicted in Figure 4.1 'it would be unreasonable to describe them as "demand curves", and reasonable to look elsewhere for the explanation of the division of the product between wages and profits'. In Figure 4.5b equilibrium does not exist; this simply means that, if this were an empirically observed fact, the marginalist argument about a tendency towards full employment through the equalization of the investment and saving schedules would be inconsistent.[43] In these cases, notes Garegnani,

there would not be sufficient ground for arguing that the rate of interest could ensure that decisions to invest will adapt to decisions to save: nor would there be sufficient ground for arguing that aggregate demand will

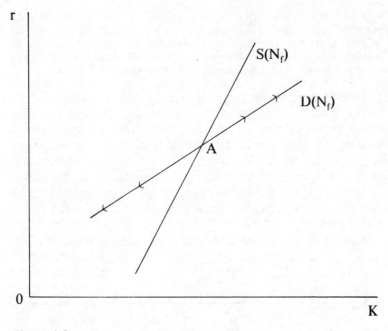

Figure 4.5a

adapt to the level of production compatible with the full employment of the
productive resources available in the economy. (1978–9, p. 41)

According to the neo-Ricardians, the effects of changes in
the rate of profit on relative prices and the choice of techniques provide the basis for a fundamental critique of the
marginalist theory of prices and output. This critique points
out to the error 'of asserting a tendency to an "equilibrium"
characterized by the full employment of labour' – an error
which is seen to be quite independent from the role of
uncertainty and expectations (Garegnani, 1977, p. 12).
Indeed, if the relation between the demand for investment
(represented by the value of capital) and the rate of profit is
not monotonic, it is not possible to conclude that there will be
a necessarily stable tendency to a situation of full employment
of labour or full utilization of the existing capital.

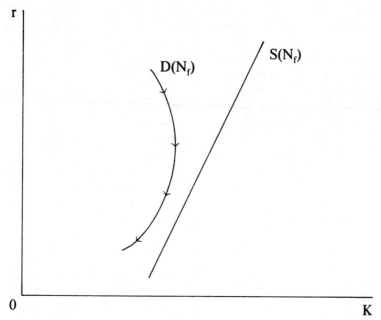

Figure 4.5b

THE ADJUSTMENT PROCESS BETWEEN SAVING AND INVESTMENT AND THE MONETARY ASPECTS OF THE NEO-RICARDIAN APPROACH

For the sake of the argument, let us put aside temporarily the implications of the capital controversy for the shape of the capital demand curve. Assume – as Keynes does in the *General Theory* – that the schedule (labelled K^d in Figures 4.6 and 4.7) is downward sloping given the inverse relation between the demand price of capital and the rate of interest. Remember that according to Keynes's construction the level of employment is not taken as given in the derivation of the capital demand curve; in fact, the levels of output and employment maintain a direct relation with the equilibrium level of investment (or stock of capital given our assumption about the circulating nature of capital). These assumptions imply that a full employment equilibrium may be attained through the equalization of the capital demand schedule and the saving curve associated with the full employment level of output. Such equilibrium exists and is stable: it may be represented by point A in Figure 4.6. However, if, for some reason, the actual or market rate of interest is persistently above the rate corresponding to the full employment equilibrium, such a position will never be attained.

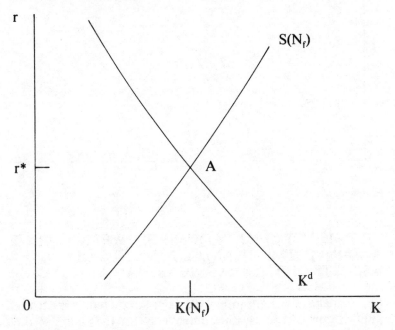

Figure 4.6

It is a well known fact that both in the *Treatise* and the *General Theory* the actual rate of interest does not depend only on saving and investment decisions. It depends on the state of liquidity preference of the economy or, what is the same, on the decisions of the various agents as to how to allocate their stock of wealth. The demand for funds to be invested and the supply of funds that have been saved play only a marginal role in the conditions of liquidity of the

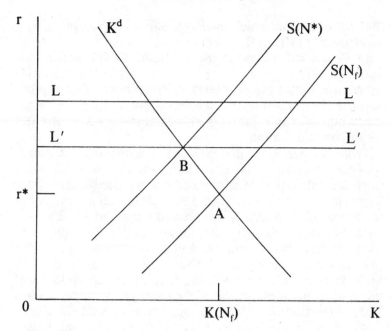

Figure 4.7

economy. They are decisions about the allocation of flows which may only affect the decisions about the allocation of stocks very marginally. In the *General Theory* the rate of interest is assumed to be only relatively dependent on the demand and supply of current funds; it depends essentially on the demand for and supply of money or, more generally, liquid assets. The rate of interest 'is the "price" which equilibrates the desire to hold wealth in the form of cash with the available quantity of cash' (JMK, VII, p. 93). The interest rate thus determined can be seen as exogenous and represented by the line LL in Figure 4.7. The existence of such a line would preclude the system from attaining the full employment equilibrium. Enter Keynes's principle of effective demand: in equilibrium, the flow of saving must correspond to the current level of investment which is, in turn, determined by the equalization of the marginal efficiency of capital and the market rate of interest. As Keynes argued, 'it is not the rate of interest, but the level of income which ensures equality between saving and investment' (JMK, VII, p. 211).

In Figure 4.7 a new saving schedule, S(N*), and a new liquidity preference curve L'L', both corresponding to a level of income smaller than the level compatible with full employment, intersect the investment schedule (point B). Equilibrium exists and is stable but it does not correspond to the full employment of labour.

From the neo-Ricardian point of view the above explanation for the possibility of equilibrium *cum* unemployment provides only a partial critique of the marginalist approach. The principle of effective demand is clearly an alternative to the marginalist theory of output and employment. But neo-Ricardians argue that Keynes's theory of interest coupled with the downward investment demand curve left open a door for the marginalist resurgence.[44] Falling money wages, through their effect on the price level and, therefore, on the liquidity of the system, or an expansion of the money supply, can always make the actual rate converge to the rate associated with the full employment of labour. In terms of Figure 4.7, this means that point B is not a stable position, and the principle of effective demand, therefore, is not inconsistent with a long-period tendency towards the full employment position.

According to the neo-Ricardian view, the cause of unemployment in Keynes's model should not be associated with the rigidity of money wages.[45] Neo-Ricardians recognize that a reduction in money wages has ambiguous effects on the level of employment (as noted by Keynes in chapter 19 of the *General Theory*) but they insist that the *real differentia* between Keynes's approach and the traditional approach is due to differences in their theories of the interest rate.[46] However, Keynes's theory of the rate of interest does not totally meet this requirement; that is, according to the neo-Ricardian argument, the rate of interest, as determined in Keynes's theory of liquidity preference, is not really independent from discrepancies between investment and full employment saving in the long period.

In the *General Theory*, expectations concerning the future path of the interest rate and the 'normal' level of the interest rate play a major part in the determination of today's rate. The fact that expectations are volatile and exogenously determined makes the liquidity preference theory a *short-period* theory of the rate of interest. Moreover, the theory depends on the agents' view as to what is the 'normal' or 'safe' rate of interest – something that the theory does not explain:[47]

Keynes's theory appears therefore to rest on the assumption of a considerable degree of stability of the expectations concerning the rate of interest: a stability which can only be based on stable views . . . as to what constitutes a 'normal' level of the interest rate. Yet when it is interpreted in this way, the inadequacy of the liquidity preference theory as a long-period analysis of the rate of interest becomes even clearer; the average value, over time, of the rate of interest . . . proves to be largely determined by views about the 'normal' rate of interest, views which the theory does not explain. (Garegnani, 1978–9, p. 53)[48]

However, in the long period, if wages keep falling as long as there is unemployment, the rate of interest will eventually start falling; and if the investment demand function is inversely related to the rate of interest, the system will gradually converge to a position of full employment.[49] Thus, Keynes's liquidity preference theory does not seem to present an alternative to the traditional (or Wicksellian) theory.

Keynes himself was quite confident that his theory of the interest rate provided an explanation for the determination of the rate of interest in the short and long periods:

it cannot be held that the position towards which the economic system is tending or the position at which it would be at rest . . ., whichever of these tendencies we have in view, is entirely independent of the policy of the monetary authority; whilst, on the other hand, it cannot be maintained that there is a unique policy which, in the long run the monetary authority is bound to pursue. . . . On my view, there is no unique long-period position of equilibrium equally valid regardless of the character of the monetary authority. On the contrary there are a number of such positions corresponding to different policies. (JMK, XXIX, p. 55)

The view that the rate of interest is mainly determined by the monetary authority is not inconsistent with the liquidity preference theory. Indeed, the monetary authority can fix the interest rate if it adapts the money supply to the state of liquidity preference of the community. The neo-Ricardians may be right in considering capital deepening a more fundamental cause of unemployment than the 'rigidity' of the interest rate. Monetary authorities can always force the interest rate down, and take the economy to a full employment position. But there is little they can do if the cause of unemployment is the particular shape of the capital employment curve which, after all, depends on the characteristics of the technology in use.[50]

Although the neo-Ricardians do not emphasize Keynes's own view on the long-period nature of the determination of the rate of interest in his liquidity preference theory, they do recognize that

it would be a mistake to conclude . . . that liquidity-preference theory cannot be combined with an explanation of the 'normal' level of the rate of interest . . . such alternative would appear to be entailed in remarks made by Keynes himself: 'the rate of interest is a highly conventional [. . .] phenomenon [and] the level established by convention . . . [can be influenced by] a modest measure of persistence and consistency of purpose by the monetary authority (JMK, vol. VII, pp. 235–44)'. (Milgate, 1982, p. 96)

In the work of Pivetti (1985, 1988) and Panico (1985, 1988) the notion that the monetary authority can fix the rate of interest is expanded and turned into an argument to substantiate Sraffa's conception in *Commodities by Means of Commodities* that the long-period rate of profit is 'susceptible of being determined from outside the system of production, in particular by the level of the money rates of interest' (Sraffa, p. 33).[51] The work of Pivetti and Panico is a clear recognition that the liquidity preference approach may provide an adequate basis for a theory of the rate of interest and the rate of profit in the long period. The discussion by neo-Ricardians of aspects associated with Keynes's monetary theory and the role of monetary institutions shows that there is a place in their research programme for these issues.

Contrary to the classical and marginalist theories, in Keynes's analysis in the *General Theory* it is the rate of interest which determines the rate of return over real capital (the 'marginal efficiency of capital'), and not the other way around:

Instead of the marginal efficiency of capital determining the rate of interest, it is truer . . . to say that it is the rate of interest which determines the marginal efficiency of capital. (JMK, VII, p. 123)

Both Panico and Pivetti emphasize the notion that the rate of interest is determined outside the sphere of production, and therefore is independent of the rate of profit. The rate of interest is determined by the state of liquidity preference, the monetary policy followed by the monetary authorities, the management of the public debt and, depending on the degree of financial openness of the economy, on the rate of interest as determined in the international financial markets. In Pivetti's (1985, p. 81) words,

interest rate policy, both in the short and in the long run, does not appear to be constrained by a somehow pre-determined normal profitability of capital. Our view then is that the rate of interest should be regarded as a 'monetary phenomenon', meaning however by this that in the causal relationship between the rate of interest and the rate of profit it is the former which 'sets the pace'.

In Panico's formulation, the interest rate over loans constitutes part of the costs of production of the firms in the productive sector, and thus enters the price equations as an additional factor:[52]

$$p = R \, p'A + bw + qi \qquad (4.9)$$

where i is the rate of interest, and q is the credit input vector, that is, 'the amount of loans in money terms per unit of product of each industry' (Panico, 1988, p. 187). The system has now n equations and $n + 2$ variables ($n - 1$ relative prices, the rate of interest, the rate of profit and the real wage). Panico adds an additional price equation for the banking system. It is assumed that the banking system uses inputs from the industrial firms, that in accordance with the assumption of competition it applies the uniform rate of profit over material costs, and that its receipts are derived from loans to the industrial firms. The banking system equation can be written as follows:

$$vi = R \, \mathbf{p}' \mathbf{a}_b + b_b \, w \qquad (4.10)$$

where v is the given total volume of loans, $\mathbf{a}_b$ is the material input vector of the banking sector, and b_b is the labour coefficient of the banking sector. The system now has $n + 1$ equations and $n + 2$ variables. If the rate of interest is determined in the monetary sphere (independently of what happens in the productive sphere), all variables of the model are determined. In this model, the relative prices and the two distributive variables (the rate of profit and the real wage) are endogenously determined.

In Pivetti's formulation, the given rate of interest and what he refers to as the normal remuneration of enterprise (the 'profit of enterprise') together determine the rate of profits:

> The normal rate of profit cannot be regarded as being strictly determined by the rate of interest. In the explanation of distribution under discussion it is necessary to take into consideration also the profit of enterprise, and by so doing the normal rate of profit . . . will be arrived at by adding up two autonomous components: the long-run rate of interest . . . or 'pure' remuneration of capital, plus the normal profit of enterprise . . . or the remuneration for the 'risk and trouble' of productively employing capital . . . (Pivetti, 1985, pp. 86–7)

Once the latter is determined, the real wage and the relative prices can be endogenously determined.

The work of Panico and Pivetti suggests that the neo-Ricardians seem to recognize that the long-period rate of interest can indeed be determined in the monetary sphere. It becomes legitimate to ask therefore how does the system adjust to a situation of disequilibrium when the rate of interest is at such a level that there is a discrepancy between the demand and supply of funds. Figure 4.8 depicts a situation in which the value of capital corresponding to the full employment of labour $(D(N_f))$ is smaller than the amount of funds forthcoming at the given rate of interest $(i = i)$.

We have seen that, according to the analysis of the *General*

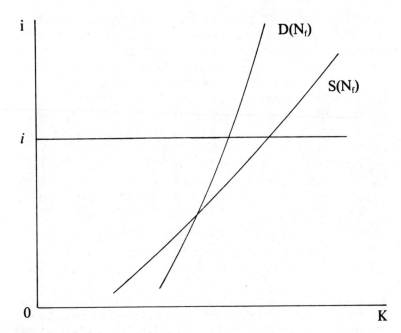

Figure 4.8

Theory, in a situation of this type the levels of output and income would fall, and the saving function would shift to the left (refer to Figure 4.7). The investment function would not move, and in the new equilibrium there would be unemployed labour.

It is quite difficult to imagine what would be the adjustment process in the neo-Ricardian formulation. Indeed, the analysis of short-run adjustment processes of this type is quite foreign to their agenda. We would suggest, however, that there are some problems associated with an attempt to conduct this analysis. Unless these problems are dealt with in a rigorous way, they could seriously undermine the neo-Ricardian claim according to which their 'critique of the conception of capital underlying [the marginalist analysis] may provide better support than was provided by Keynes himself for establishing the principle of effective demand' (Garegnani, 1979, p. 72). In other words, in order to provide this support to the notion that it is the level of income (rather than the rate of interest) which is the relevant adjustment variable for discrepancies between saving and investment, the neo-Ricardians must provide an analysis of the short-run dynamics of the adjustment process. The problems with the adjustment process in the neo-Ricardian formulation are essentially associated with the effect of changes in the level of activity on the output vector and the matrix of technical coefficients. These effects are not discussed in the neo-Ricardian literature but should not be neglected. It is quite difficult to know what would be the effect on the output vector, that is, the change in the volumes of each commodity produced and the sectoral composition of output. As for the **A** matrix, in the case of the existence of fixed capital, it would necessarily change due to changes in the degree of capacity utilization in each industry.[53]

A change in the **X** vector and the **A** matrix necessarily implies that both the value of capital curve and the saving curve will shift.[54] The questions then are: in which direction will they shift, and will the system ever converge to a situation in which the two curves together intersect the interest rate line? These seem to be very difficult analytical questions. Their answers require at least the specification of a multi-sectoral demand function relating changes in the composition of demand to changes in relative prices and the level of activity; and a dynamic system relating changes in the investment and supply curves to changes in the rate of interest. Finally, the stability condition of this system would have to be studied.

In sum, in a system in which the rate of interest is given exogenously, and the level of income is the relevant adjustment variable for discrepancies between the capital-employment and the savings curves, the adjustment process involves changes in the output vector and the A matrix which complicate considerably the analysis of the workings of the principle of effective demand. If the neo-Ricardians cannot provide a convincing analysis of the process of adjustment and the stability conditions of the system, their claim of a superior version of Keynes's principle of effective demand could be seriously undermined.

CONCLUDING REMARKS

The neo-Ricardian approach to the economics of Keynes is based on a solid research programme in which the notion of long-period position as characterized by uniform rates of profit across sectors and normal utilization of capacity plays an important part. Eatwell and Milgate do provide an interesting interpretation for Keynes's assumption of a given stock of capital, claiming that the assumption refers to the Marshallian stationary state rather than the short period. This interpretation could lead to an extension of Keynes's model in which not only stationary equilibrium positions were considered but also steady state equilibrium situations. This, however, would require the development of a neo-Ricardian theory of investment and accumulation – something that, as noted above, the neo-Ricardians have refused to do.

Neo-Ricardians claim to have provided a definite critique of the marginalist theory of distribution and employment by showing the possibility of a non-monotonic relation between the rate of interest and the value of capital. The critique, however, is not free from caveats. One basic problem is that it places too much emphasis on the shape of the investment demand schedule. Yet it is not impossible to have an upward-rising investment demand schedule compatible with a stable equilibrium associated with the full employment of labour. Figure 4.9 depicts this case.

A second problem is that the neo-Ricardian construction assumes uniform rates of profit across sectors. This assumption only holds in the long period. In the short period the composition of the stock of capital will be compatible with the composition of demand only by coincidence; therefore, only by coincidence there will be a uniform rate of profit across sectors of production. This leads us to another problem already mentioned, namely the lack of a discussion of adjustment processes in which the roles of competition, expectations and stability conditions are seriously discussed.

A third problem is that the neo-Ricardian derivation of the capital–employment curve usually assumes the level and structure of output to be given. It therefore neglects the effects on

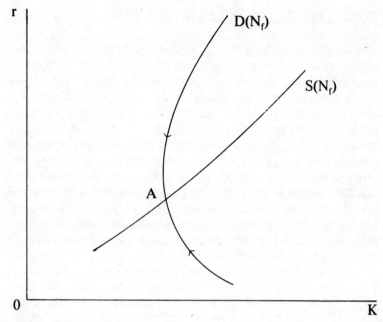

Figure 4.9

the level of output of changes in the rate of interest, that is, of changes in the distribution of income. If this effect were taken into account the shape of the capital–employment curve and the saving curve would obviously be affected. The discussion of the effect of changes in the level of activity on the output vector and the matrix of technical coefficients is certainly lacking in the neo-Ricardian approach to the principle of effective demand.[55]

A final problem with the neo-Ricardian construction as a critique of marginalist theory is that the capital–employment curve is the outcome of the Sraffian general equilibrium system, and, as such, it embodies very few behavioural assumptions on the part of the economic agents. The curve simply reflects the value of the stock of capital associated with different rates of profit. This curve cannot be compared with Keynes's marginal efficiency theory of investment demand or any other theory embodying behavioural assumptions for that matter.

Even if we ignore the problems associated with the uniformity of the rate of profits and lack of a short-period analysis, the givenness of the level of output and lack of behavioural assumptions underlying the derivation of the capital–employment curve, and concentrate on the argument about the shape of the schedule, it should be clear that the neo-Ricardians only provide a 'possibility argument'. The possibility that the equilibrium does not exist (Figure 4.5b) or is unstable (Figure 4.5a). In principle, however, the argument can be falsified (Figure 4.9). Indeed, it can be empirically falsified. What if it was? What if the empirically observed general equilibrium relation between the value of capital and the rate of profit yields a demand schedule for capital consistent with a full employment stable equilibrium? Only one alternative would then seem possible, namely to accept the marginalist view that the economy would persistently gravitate around full employment if distortions did not prevent it from doing so!

NOTES

1. A group of Italian economists, most notably Ciccone, Committeri, Panico, Pivetti and Vianello, have also contributed to this research programme. In Germany, Kurz has also contributed to the development of the neo-Ricardian approach to the economics of Keynes.
2. Both motivations are justified on the basis of the inconsistencies of the marginalist theories of value, distribution and output based on aggregate production functions. We shall return to this point presently.
3. Of course, there are other approaches to classical political economy; see, e.g., Hollander (1987).
4. All page citations of Garegnani (1978–9) refer to the reprint in Eatwell and Milgate (1983).
5. See Milgate (1982, 1988) for a review of Wicksell's analysis of saving and investment.
6. An examination of the marginalist approach is developed in the section entitled 'The Neo-Ricardian critique of marginalist money'. The neo-Ricardian claim according to which the marginalist analysis of the relation between saving and investment is potentially inconsistent is based on the fact that in a model with heterogeneous commodities, the equilibrium between saving and investment may not exist, or if it exists, might not be stable.
7. In neo-Ricardian texts it is argued that the investment function must be negatively sloped which is a sufficient but definitely not a necessary

condition for the system to be stable. We shall return to this point presently.

8. See Harcourt (1972) for a detailed examination of the main issues and results of the capital controversy.

9. Not only the stability of the system but also the existence and uniqueness of the equilibrium position depend on the slope of the investment function.

10. This does not mean that the neo-Ricardians do not see any value in Keynes's theory of the rate of interest. In fact, Panico (1988) and Pivetti (1985) take Keynes's approach as a starting point for their theory of the determination of the long-run rates of interest and profit.

11. Neo-Ricardians prefer the term 'long period positions' rather than 'equilibrium positions'. The reason for this is that the classical theory of value and distribution (based on which the neo-Ricardian contributions are developed) does not 'resort to the "opposite forces of supply and demand" ' which implies that the 'word "equilibrium" does not seem appropriate to describe the position of the economic system characterized by 'natural' prices, wages and profits' (Garegnani, 1976, p. 130, n. 2). In the text, however, we shall refer to equilibrium and disequilibrium positions rather than long and short periods; we shall restrict the usage of the terms long and short periods to their Marshallian meaning – to be defined in the text. Also, neo-Ricardians are reluctant to accept the conventional association of long-period positions with steady state situations; we shall have the opportunity to return to this aspect of the neo-Ricardian approach presently.

12. The concept of stability being considered here should be distinguished from the standard one according to which stability is associated with the notion of convergence of the system.

13. See Garegnani (1984, pp. 295–7) for the definition of 'core' and the specification of the core in the neo-Ricardian system.

14. See Dutt (1986).

15. From a logical point of view the first and second reasons seem to provide a reasonable justification for considering the money wage parametrically in the *General Theory's* system. First, there are institutional factors determining the wage which may be stronger than the conditions of supply and demand for labour. Second, the effect of changes in money wages on the endogenous variables (employment and distribution) is highly ambiguous.

16. For models in which the long-period or equilibrium degree of capacity utilization may diverge from the desired degree, see Amadeo (1987b, 1988) and Dutt (1984, 1987a, 1989).

17. According to Bharadwaj (1985, pp. 19–20),

to the classicals, competition signified mobility of capital and to a certain extent of labour, manifesting itself in a tendency towards uniformity of the rate of profit and wages. It was even allowed by Adam Smith that there could be a vector of rates of profits and wages, with more or less stable differentials, not greatly or systematically affected by the advance of the economy.

See also Dutt (1988).

18. The fact that the equilibrium position according to the neo-Ricardian approach corresponds to the Marshallian long period is also evident from the following passage by Garegnani:

> [l]ong-period theory analyses what will happen *over an average* of such 'short periods', when, with the possibility of changes in the size of plant, the effects of such incongruities [between the stock of capital and demand] will tend to cancel each other out. (1979b, p. 76, emphasis added)

19. See Amadeo's (1987b) comments on Ciccone's analysis.
20. In the section entitled 'The Neo-Ricardian critique of marginalist theory' we discuss the determination of relative prices and the distribution of income using the Sraffian system.
21. Bharadwaj notes that the fact that the level and composition of output, the methods of production and the real wage are taken as givens does not mean that the interaction among 'levels of output (and changes therein), distribution, and technology' should not be considered in the analysis, but that

> such interrelations are considered diverse and complex enough (so that historical specificities and regularities may not be (ignored) to require deeper analysis outside the domain of the price determination . . . [t]his implies . . . a separation of the analysis . . . of quantities and prices. (1985, pp. 8–9)

22. See Garegnani (1978–9), Eatwell (1983) and Milgate (1982).
23. See, e.g., Hahn (1982).
24. See Dutt (1988).
25. According to Garegnani, 'incorrect price expectations entertained in the past might indeed be a way of describing some of the factors that make the market prices deviate from the natural prices' (1976, p. 133). Again:

> It seems . . . that the 'accidental causes' which were traditionally thought to make actual or 'market' prices deviate from their long-period levels, could be described in terms of incorrect expectations. And just the incorrectness of these expectations, i.e. their contrast with subsequent experience, was supposed to lead to their progressive revision as a part of the process by which the economy tends to the equilibrium or, more generally, the 'long-period position' corresponding to the given conditions. (Garegnani, 1979, p. 7)

As for the role of uncertainty in the *General Theory*, according to Garegnani,

> Keynes argued that uncertainty about the future, acting both through the volatility of the expectations controlling investment and through liquidity preference, would prevent investment from tending to the level set by full employment saving. This notion of the role of uncertainty was formulated by Keynes in the context of the short period in which capital equipment is given but he evidently thought that its consequences went further. (1977, p. 8)

26. In this respect the *General Theory* departs from other post-Wicksellian contributions (including Keynes's *Treatise*) in which short-period expectations play quite a central role in determining the path of the system over a series of short periods. In these analyses the notion of equilibrium position is relegated to a second place. See Amadeo (1989).

27. Perhaps we should be more careful about this statement. Post Keynesians would suggest that due to the role of changing long-period expectations the equilibrium would be continuously moving. Keynes himself could argue that the *General Theory*, rather than based on a stationary equilibrium method, is a 'theory of shifting equilibrium – meaning [by this] the theory of a system in which changing views about the future are capable of influencing the present situation' (JMK, VII, p. 293). Other Keynesians such as Leijohnfvud would argue that

> Keynes used the term 'unemployment equilibrium' . . . [But] . . . it is not an equilibrium in the strict sense at all. It is preferable to use some more neutral terms which does not carry the connotation that no equilibrating forces at all are at work. The real question is why the forces tending to bring the system back to full employment are so weak. (1968, p. 22)

28. The following analysis of Eatwell and Milgate's claim follows Amadeo (1989, ch. 8).

29. See Asimakopulos (1985, 1986) for a criticism of Eatwell and Milgate. Harcourt and O'Shaughnessy (1985) argue that Eatwell and Milgate's interpretation of the *General Theory* lacks textual evidence.

30. In examining Eatwell and Milgate's interpretation, Bhattacharjea (1987) also comes to the conclusion that, in fact, Keynes's *General Theory* is essentially concerned with Marshall's short period.

31. In fact, Eatwell and Milgate's interpretation is also inspired by Robinson (1937, ch. 5). See Eatwell (1983) and Amadeo (1989).

32. See Dutt (1989, chapters 6 and 7) for alternative two-sector models and Marglin (1984, chapter 11) for an n-commodity long-period model with classical and Keynesian closures.

33. See Pasinetti (1977) for a clear presentation of this point.

34. The orthodox or marginalist elements of Keynes's *General Theory*, according to the neo-Ricardians, are the marginal efficiency of capital curve which maintains a negative relation with the rate of interest, and the demand curve for labour which maintains a negative relation with the real wage.
35. See also Eatwell (1977) and Kurz (1985).
36. By assumption, the commodity serves two purposes: that of capital good and that of consumption good. In the following analysis, we shall assume that all capital is circulating capital which implies that capital and investment in each period are conceptually equal.
37. In the Sraffian or neo-Ricardian system, one distributive variable (usually the rate of profit), the methods of production (the coefficients a_{ij} and b_i) and the level and sectoral composition of output are exogenously given. In the simple two-sector system we are discussing, the real wage and the relative price are endogenously determined. In general, that is, in a system with n commodities, the real wage and the n-1 relative prices are endogenously determined.
38. The system has n equations and n + 1 variables (the real wage, the profit rate and n-1 relative prices). When we fix the rate of profit, the system becomes determined.
39. See Pasinetti (1977, p. 88).
40. Pasinetti (1977, p. 87) discusses the conditions for the independence of relative prices in relation to changes in the rate of profits in the general n-commodity case.
41. See Garegnani (1970), Pasinetti (1977) and Harris (1978).
42. The extent to which this analogy is legitimate depends on how one interprets the different assumptions behind each curve. In the homogeneous commodity case, it is assumed that there is continuous substitution between labour and capital, decreasing marginal returns and profit maximization. In the neo-Ricardian construction – the case of heterogeneous capital goods – the extent to which there is 'substitution' between the factors of production depends on the number of techniques available, and for each technique, fixed coefficients are assumed which implies that the notion of marginal returns does not make any sense. The only point in common is the assumption of an optimizing behaviour on the part of producers.
43. It is interesting to note that Keynes in his critique of the classical theory of interest (chapter 14 of the *General Theory*) refers to the possibility of the non-existence of equilibrium based on the argument that the saving function may be negatively sloped. He there argues:

it has been agreed . . . that it is not certain that the sum saved out of a given income necessarily increases when the rate of interest is increased; whereas no one doubts that investment demand-schedules fall with a rising interest rate. But if the Y-curves [saving schedules] and the X-curves [investment schedules] both fall as the rate of interest rises, there is no guarantee that a given Y-curve will intersect a given X-curve anywhere at all. (p. 182)

44. According to Garegnani (1978-9, p. 60),

the idea of an investment demand schedule constitutes an obstacle which a monetary theory of interest cannot easily overcome. Indeed, admitting an [downward] elastic investment demand schedule leads to maintaining, on the one hand, the existence of a full employment level of the rate of interest and, on the other, the presence of inflation or deflation and unemployment, when the actual rate of interest is not the full employment one; the idea that the market rate of interest tends to gravitate towards its full employment level then acquires plausibility.

45. Thus, Garegnani notes that

the hypothesis of money wage rigidity does not suffice to explain the difference between Keynes's conclusions and those of the traditional economists; the flexibility of prices and wages would lead to the full employment of factors *only if* the resulting decrease in the rate of interest could so affect planned investment as to make it equal to full employment saving. (1978-9, p. 50)

46. Hence the only relevant long-period effect of changes in money wages according to the neo-Ricardians is the effect on the rate of interest. See Garegnani (1978-9, p. 50), and Milgate (1982, ch. VII).

47. Thus, Milgate argues that

if the rate of interest is determined by reference to views about its 'safe' or . . . 'normal' level, then the application of liquidity-preference in long-period analysis is highly questionable, for liquidity-preference does not explain just what needs to be explained there – that 'normal' rate itself. Indeed, by running in short-period terms the presence of liquidity-preference theory has provided . . . a basis for reasserting the orthodox position . . . (1982, p. 95)

48. Bhattacharjea (1987) argues that Keynes did have a long-period theory of the rate of interest in the *General Theory*. He suggests that even if there was no speculative demand for money, the 'essential properties of money' would imply the existence of a floor for the rate of interest, and therefore would impose a limit on the potential effects of a deflation of wages and prices on investment. The essential properties of money (that is, zero elasticity of substitution and the inelasticity of supply) give rise to an inflexible 'liquidity premium' which, according to Bhattacharjea's interpretation, 'is endemic to the normal operation of the economy, not necessarily disappearing in the longest run' (p. 279). However, Bhattacharjea tends to agree that the neo-Ricardian fundamental criticism of the marginalist theory of capital is essentially

correct, and is independent of their view on Keynes's theory of interest.
49. See Garegnani (1978-9, p. 55).
50. As a matter of fact, we shall argue in chapter 6 that the rigidity of the interest rate could be a result rather than a cause of unemployment if unemployment were, in fact, a consequence of capital reversal or reswitching.
51. In his 1978-9 paper, Garegnani notes that

> Keynes's suggestion that the average rate of interest on long-term loans will be determined by conventional factors, ultimately subject to the policy of the monetary authorities (Keynes, 1936, pp. 203-4), would suffice to constitute the nucleus of a theory of distribution. Indeed, it seems reasonable to suppose that, as a result of competition in product markets, the average rate of profits and the average rate of interest on long-term loans will tend, over a sufficiently long period, to move in step with one another. If, then, the rate of interest depends on the policy of the monetary authorities, both the long-term movement of the average rate of profit and . . . that of real wages are explained by this policy. (p. 63)

This suggestion by Garegnani seems to have prompted the discussion of the relation between monetary policy, the rate of interest and the rate of profit in the neo-Ricardian literature.
52. The system presented in the text is a simplified version of Panico's formulation.
53. In a model with fixed capital, the a_{ij} coefficients will change when the level of activity changes.
54. In the text we assumed that the volume of saving is a positive function of the rate of interest and the level of employment. This assumption avoids considerations over the effect of changes in relative prices on income. However, in general, a change in the rate of interest will affect the value of the volume of output produced in each industry and thus income and saving.
55. If we introduce capacity utilization, it is possible that Sraffa's apparatus will come into question. See Dutt (1986, 1989).

5. The Post Keynesians

INTRODUCTION

A number of Keynesian economists have emphasized the historical (as opposed to mechanical or logical) nature of time, the importance of uncertainty (as opposed to risk), the role of money and monetary institutions (as opposed to treating money as a veil), and the inapplicability of the equilibrium method in the study of economics, both in Keynes's work and for an adequate analysis of real economies. Some of these economists have been referred to by such names as 'Post Keynesians', 'American post Keynesians', and 'Keynesian fundamentalists',[1] while others who are normally associated with other groups have – recently – expressed similar ideas. For the purposes of this book we shall refer to the entire group as Post Keynesians.

Post Keynesianism in our sense arose almost from the time of the *General Theory*. Townshend (1937) spelt out the implications of a Keynesian analysis of uncertainty and expectation for neo-classical price theory. There have been many subsequent contributors, and the following is a rather selective listing. In a series of writings, Shackle (1938, 1955, 1967, 1972) has emphasized the nature of uncertainty described by Keynes, and its implications for decision making and the functioning of the economy. In Shackle (1982) he writes unequivocally that 'the elemental core of Keynes' conception of economic society is uncertain expectation, and uncertain expectation is wholly incompatible and in conflict with the notion of equilibrium'. Joan Robinson (1974, 1977) has repeatedly emphasized the idea of historical time in Keynes's theory, and has questioned the use of the neo-classical notion of equilibrium and stability analysis in economic theory. The trio of American Post Keynesians – Davidson (1972), S. Weintraub (1958) and Wells (1979b) – have focused on the role of money and uncertainty in the *General Theory*, and argued that unemployment could occur only in a monetary economy, and any reasonable macroeconomic theory would have to incorporate money and uncertainty in an appropriate manner, something not done in neo-classical theory. This trio, and others including Asimakopulos (1982), Chick (1983), Kregel (1976), and Tarshis (1979), have emphasized the role of expectations formation using a Marshallian short-period notion, thereby emphasizing the role of historical time. Kaldor (1982) [see also Kaldor and Trevithick (1981)] has emphasized the endogeneity of money [as have Weintraub and others] in capitalist economies, and has criticized the neo-classical notion of equilibrium [see Kaldor (1972, 1985)]. Finally, Minsky (1975, 1982, 1986) has emphasized the role of the financing of investment, the role of banks, and the liability structure of businesses; his vision of the economy is that of an inherently unstable one, which cannot adequately be captured in an equilibrium model.

Apart from these, whom we would not hesitate to call Post Keynesians, similar ideas have been expressed by some who are not primarily Post Keynesian. Thus Clower (1967) has emphasized the role of money in causing the effective demand problem. Leijonhufvud (1968) has discussed the implications of price deflation for the supply of money and aggregate demand much in the same way as the Post Keynesians. Some general equilibrium theorists, such as Arrow and Hahn (1971) and Hahn (1977) have argued that if money is appropriately incorporated into an Arrow–Debreu type general equilibrium model, there would be problems in showing the existence of equilibrium. Meltzer (1981), who can be classified as a monetarist, has recently emphasized the role of expectations and money in much the same way as the other Post Keynesians, although he differentiates his product from theirs by asserting – without adequate justification – that the capitalist system is basically stable. Even Hicks (1976), the creator of the IS–LM model, a favourite whipping dog of many Post Keynesians for its timelessness, has turned against his earlier *avatar* and emphasized the role of time in Keynes's theory. Several mainstream Keynesians have now recognized that wage flexibility may not result in full employment, admitting the importance of historical time and money. Tobin (1975) argued that deflation, through its effect on the real interest rate, could discourage consumption and investment expenditure, a mechanism which Hahn and Solow (1986) have recently sought to formalize with an overlapping generations model. Weitzman (1982) and Solow (1985) have shown that a lower real wage in an economy characterized by increasing returns to scale and imperfectly competitive firms is associated with a *lower* level of employment, due to lower aggregate demand. Howitt (1986) has used a rational expectations model to show that a reduction in the money wage could reduce employment through wealth redistributions, and that greater wage flexibility could increase the variation in employment (thereby possibly raising the degree of uncertainty). Finally, Hahn (1987) has developed several models of learning behaviour to show that the equilibrium position for the market may be path-dependent, formalizing the Post Keynesian idea of the importance of history. It would be quite fair to infer that these mainstream Keynesians are beginning to accept Post Keynesian views, although they have usually been interested in formalizing one or two isolated mechanisms, and without acknowledging the contributions of the Post Keynesians.

There is no question that Keynes had a lot to say on the issues mentioned above, which have allowed the members of the group to quote extensively from his work. On uncertainty, his approach was developed very early, at least from the *Treatise on Probability*.[2] No one reading chapter 12 of the *General Theory*, or Keynes's 1937 paper responding to some comments on that book [see JMK, XIV] can doubt the importance that he placed on uncertainty. There is also no reason to believe that such issues are specific to this chapter and the paper; chapter 5 also discusses the question of short- and long-period expectations.[3] However, in chapter 11, which discusses the determinants of investment, his treatment is rather Fisherian, and uncertainty and expectations are not emphasized.[4] Regarding money, Keynes's initial exposition of the aggregate demand – aggregate supply analysis in chapter 3 does not introduce money explicitly. But he does emphasize the point that one must forsake the classical postulate of the equality of the real wage to the marginal disutility of work because the wage bargain was made in terms of the *money* wage rather than the real wage, and it need not be that a fall in the money wage resulting from unemployment would reduce the real wage, which was required for making firms increase their employment of labour. The Post Keynesians who argue that Keynes was primarily concerned with monetary economies lean heavily on chapter 17, on the essential properties of interest and money, to substantiate their claim.

This chapter reviews critically the contributions of these Post Keynesians. Since the literature is voluminous, we have to be rather selective, even regarding contributions on themes we discuss. We examine Post Keynesian ideas on time, uncertainty, money and equilibrium. The section, 'The Aggregate Demand – Aggregate Supply Model' examines a Post Keynesian model of the determination of employment following chapters 3 and 5 of the *General Theory*, and examines some Post Keynesian criticisms of other macroeconomic models. The penultimate section examines the implications of wage reductions and wage flexibility, extending the Post Keynesian model, and comments on the role of the central Post Keynesian tenets concerning time, uncertainty, money and equilibrium, in this analysis. Finally, we make some concluding comments. Prior to all this, however, we re-emphasize (see chapter 1) that we use the term in a very restricted sense. We discuss the broader definition of the term, and mention some Post Keynesian contributions in this broader sense that will not be discussed in this book, in the following section.

POST KEYNESIANS – A BROADER VIEW

Many recent discussions [see Dow (1985), Harcourt (1985, 1987a,b), and Hamouda and Harcourt (1988)] of Post Keynesian economics use the term Post Keynesian in a far broader sense than we do. These discussions include not only the neo-Ricardian Keynesians (and neo-Ricardians more generally), but also almost all economists writing on macroeconomic theory (and its microeconomic foundations) from a non-neoclassical and non-Marxist (in a fundamentalist sense) perspective.[5] As explained in chapter 1, our narrow perspective is explained by the specific purpose of this book: to understand the similarities and differences between two specific approaches to Keynes's *General Theory*. The neo-Ricardians are not included because we have already discussed their contributions in chapter 4. Many others whose contributions underline the importance of the issues emphasized in this chapter are left out because their work is not directly relevant for interpreting the *General Theory*. These contributions have tried to extend and modify Keynes's analysis by incorporating imperfect competition into the analysis, emphasizing the importance of income distribution, pursuing the dynamic implications of Keynes's analysis by studying inflation, cycles and growth, to mention only a few directions. These contributions have borrowed liberally from the work of Ricardo, Marx and Kalecki and, indeed, sometimes been closer to Kalecki than to Keynes.

The dividing line between interpreters of the *General Theory* and extenders and modifiers of Keynes is admittedly a fuzzy one. Despite the practical difficulties of distinguishing between those who are primarily interested in exploring what Keynes really meant (or should have meant) in the *General Theory* (given his objective of demonstrating the possibility of unemployment equilibrium) and those who use a Keynesian approach to study issues and situations with which Keynes was not directly interested, we believe that the distinction can in principle be made. But because the dividing line is admittedly vague, we should mention some importance issues which will *not* be discussed in this book (except perhaps for some passing mentions).

Several writers have sought to extend Keynes's theory of effective demand to incorporate imperfect competition and/or income distributional issues, very much along Kaleckian lines. Tarshis (1939) developed, independently, an approach similar to Kalecki's, and has built on these ideas over the years [see Tarshis (1947, 1948) for example]. Weintraub (1958) [see also Kregel (1985)] has also developed a similar approach.

Keynes had been concerned with the problem of unemployment. But with the emergence of inflation and stagflation, Keynes's methods have been used by the Post Keynesians to examine their causes and to suggest anti-inflation schemes. These efforts have been pioneered by Weintraub (1978a) and Lerner [see Lerner and Collander (1979)].

Although in the *General Theory* Keynes did devote a chapter to the study of the business cycle, this was more an attempt at the application of his theory of unemployment equilibrium rather than at developing a theory of business cycles as such. Several writers have extended Keynes's analysis to develop the theory of business cycles, including Hicks (1950), Samuelson (1939), Kaldor (1940), Goodwin (1951, 1967), Pasinetti (1974) and Minsky (1982, 1986), sometimes incorporating factors such as the accelerator mechanism and financial issues that were not present in Keynes's own discussion. Kalecki (1954, 1971) of course, developed his own theories of the cycle extending his own models of effective demand.[6]

Finally, the analysis has been extended to deal with issues relating to capital accumulation and growth over the long run. These, owing much to Kalecki (1954, 1971) and Marx as well, were undertaken by Harrod (1939), Steindl (1952), Baran and Sweezy (1966), Robinson (1956, 1962), Pasinetti (1962) and Kaldor (1957). Kaldor's own theories often tended to assume full employment of labour in long-run growth equilibrium (he also had problems in showing how the economy achieved full employment), so that they were removed from the Keynesian theories of effective-demand constrained growth with unemployment.[7]

These contributions, together with others that would have to be included if we were to interpret Post Keynesianism even more broadly, will not be discussed in this chapter, except in passing. A fairly exhaustive survey is available in Hamouda and Harcourt (1988), and shorter accounts can be found in Harcourt (1985, 1987b).

TIME IN POST KEYNESIAN ECONOMICS

Concerning time in economics, the Post Keynesians treat it as historical time, rather than mechanical or logical time as in neo-classical economic theory, and in the neo-Ricardian approach for that matter. Joan Robinson has been one of the most forceful expositors of this view.[8] A clear exposition of the problem is due to Hicks (1976), who argues against the analogy between time and space often made in economics. He writes:

> In space we can move either way, or any way; but time just goes on, never goes back. We represent time on our diagram by a spatial coordinate; but the representation is never a complete representation; it always leaves something out . . . It is quite hard to get away, in any part of our thinking, from the spatial representation . . . One of the principal consequences of the irreversibility of time is that past and future are different . . . The past . . . cannot be changed. [It] . . ., however, has this virtue that we can have knowledge of it, knowledge of fact. The knowledge that we have, or can have, of the past is different in kind from what we know of the future; for the latter, at best, is no more a knowledge of probabilities. (Hicks, 1982, p. 283)

Robinson (1974) refers to the concept of time which takes into account the fact that its movement involves a move from an irreversible past to an uncertain future, historical time. This can be contrasted to two other notions of time, which are commonly used in neo-classical economics. One is the notion of mechanical time, which is reversible; in it, as Dow (1985, p. 113) writes, 'the transition from one state to the next can be precisely reversed'. The other is logical time [see Termini (1981)], which does not actually involve the passage of time but refers to logical precedence in a causal sequence: the exogenous variables in a simultaneous system of equations come before, in logical time, the endogenous variables.[9] Logical time can be thought of as Hicks's (1979) notion of contemporaneous causality, that is, in terms of an equilibrium setting. Mechanical time can be thought of in terms of comparative statics in the usual sense, where a parametric change takes us to one position, and reversing that parametric change takes us back to the original position.

Note that irreversibility and uncertainty are both important for not being able to collapse historical time into mechanical or logical time. In the absence of uncertainty (or in the presence of a complete set of future markets) any economy in time can be reduced legitimately into a static general equilibrium system. We should also add that if time were reversible, uncertainty would be of no consequence. If decisions are completely reversible, mistakes could be reversed, and final equilibrium positions can be studied by treating time as being mechanical.

There is no question that economic activity involves many decisions which are irreversible (to a considerable degree). For example, production takes time and once the process is begun often difficult or impossible to reverse; investment gives rise to productive capacity in the future, which cannot be easily removed; and the purchase of assets results in income in the future. Even if it is possible physically to reverse these processes and activities, it is not possible to go back in time and obliterate them altogether; their effects will affect the actors in the future. The decision makers must take into account this irreversibility of time in all decision making.

There are two separate issues here: how do individuals behave with the knowledge that time is historical and how should economic analysis be altered to take this into account? and should economic analysis necessarily impose that the economy actually tends to a state that depends on the course of history, in other words, must it model in some way the irreversibility of time? One can do the former without doing the latter, by modelling economic behaviour as if the past was irrevocable, without actually introducing irrevocability into the analysis.[10] The former issue can be thought of as trying to model the behaviour of individuals while maintaining the equilibrium and comparative statics devices. The latter interpretation should also introduce some irreversibilities into the analysis. Examples could be a ratchet effect in consumption or wages, or in the nature of expectation formation, or in the stock of capital.

Post Keynesian analysis has tried to deal with historical time by carefully analysing the passage of time in its analyses.

Chick (1983, pp. 16–21) examines in detail different time horizons that are involved in production, consumption, saving and investment decisions, and shows how they are related to Keynes's notions of 'short-period' and 'long-period' expectations. Keynes was following the Marshallian method of considering market, short and long periods, to deal with time. Most of the Post Keynesian discussion along these lines refers to the behaviour of individuals and firms under uncertainty in different time horizons, to which we will turn in the next section. Regarding the modelling of irrevocability, or path dependent equilibria, irreversibility concerning capital stock (which was hidden under the rug by the neo-classical treatment of capital as perfectly shiftable putty) is not relevant for the discussion of the short run as understood here. Some discussion of ratchet effects in wage changes is available in the Post Keynesian literature [see Chick (1983, pp. 160–1)], but path-dependent equilibrium has not been discussed much, although it would seem to be highly relevant to the notion of historical time. Hahn (1987) has formalized such a process, however, in which an imperfectly competitive profit-maximizing firm, uncertain of his demand curve, learns from actual outcomes of prices and quantities, and revises probabilities in a Bayesian manner when this new information arrives. The final equilibrium is shown to depend on the starting point, implying the path-dependence of equilibrium. It should be possible to model such path-dependence within a Post Keynesian perspective, without using Hahn's neo-classical assumptions and individual maximizing behaviour.[11] We will return to this theme when we consider its implications for equilibrium analysis, in the section entitled 'Equilibrium and Post Keynesian economics'.

UNCERTAINTY AND POST KEYNESIAN ECONOMICS

Post Keynesians give uncertainty a central role in Keynesian economics. They argue that economic agents live in an uncertain environment, so that they can at most have subjective ideas about the likely outcomes of their decisions. Neo-classical economics, by treating uncertainty as risk, essentially reduces uncertainty to certainty. To understand how uncertainty affects economic behaviour Post Keynesians have gone back to Keynes's ideas on probability and uncertainty which, despite their persuasiveness, have been ignored in mainstream economic theory.

Since Post Keynesians refer extensively to Keynes's own writings on these themes, it makes sense to begin with a discussion of these. In fact Keynes's ideas on these matters began to take shape long before the *General Theory*, and Post Keynesian writers have recently devoted a great deal of attention to these earlier writings.[12] It has been argued [see Carabelli (1985, 1988) and O'Donnell (1982), for example] that Keynes's ideas on these issues showed an essential continuity. In the *Treatise on Probability* (JMK, VIII) Keynes shifted the discussion of cause and chance from explanation by material and physical connections to the study of the processes of knowing and believing. For him, probability consisted of a logical relation between propositions, and depended on the amount of knowledge available in a world of limited knowledge. People act with limited knowledge, but not with ignorance. With low knowledge, additional information about something will increase, if not the probability, the 'weight' of the argument. Keynes distinguishes his approach from the approach which used the atomic hypothesis, with which scientists studied natural phenomena. According to this hypothesis, the material universe consisted of

legal atoms, such that each of them exercises its own, separate, independent, invariable effects, a change of the total state being compounded of a number of separated changes each of which is solely due to a separate portion of the preceding state . . . Each atom can, according to this theory, be treated as a separate cause and thus not enter into different organic compositions in each of which it is regulated by different laws. (JMK, VIII, pp. 276-7)

This is the hypothesis which allowed the application of the calculus of probability and the techniques of statistical inference. For Keynes a 'degree of probability is not composed of some homogeneous material, and is apparently not divisible into parts of like character with one another' [JMK, VIII, p.

32]. Whatever the status of the atomic hypothesis in the natural sciences, Keynes's view was that it was not valid for the world of social relations, where we have 'the problems of organic unity, of discreteness, of discontinuity – the whole is not equal to the sum of the parts, comparisons of quantity fail us' [JMK, X, p. 262]. Given this organic dependence and the resulting uniqueness of phenomena, Keynes based his notion of probability on ordinary language and common sense rather than on analytical terms; and it was not possible to attach numerical magnitudes to probabilities in any objective way.[13]

These ideas were carried over to Keynes's later works, especially to the *General Theory*; the ideas were also extended in several directions. In these works he went from the general discussion on probability and uncertainty to the specifics regarding the uncertainty facing economic agents. Although there is some discussion of uncertainty and expectation formation in the discussion of production, most of it has to do with investment and asset holding decisions. Regarding the firm, Keynes distinguished, as already mentioned, between short- and long-run expectations. The former concerned expected proceeds from production and sales employing the existing capital stock and the latter concerned the future profitability of investment. It was to the latter, and therefore to the investment decision, that Keynes paid the most attention in his discussion of uncertainty. In the first chapter on investment (chapter 11), as mentioned above, he considers investment behaviour as if investors could form numerical measures of expected returns; here although his notion of uncertainty hides (though not very well) below the surface, the analysis is rather Fisherine. But in chapter 12, entitled 'The State of Long-Term Expectations', uncertainty enters centre stage, and makes investment behaviour largely autonomous, dependent primarily on animal spirits. He writes that the 'outstanding fact is the extreme precariousness of the basis of knowledge on which our estimates of prospective yield have to be made' (JMK, VII, 149). This uncertainty, as he makes clear in his 1937 paper, 'The General Theory of Employment', was very different from situations where repeated experiments could be performed and observed:

By 'uncertain' knowledge, let me explain, I do not merely distinguish between what is known for certain from what is only probable. The game of roulette is not subject, in this sense, to uncertainty; nor is the prospect of a Victory bond being drawn . . . The sense in which I am using the term is that in which the prospect of a European war is uncertain . . . About these matters there is no scientific basis on which to form any calculable probability whatever. We simply do not know. (JMK, XIV, pp. 113–14)

Yet for making investment decisions investors would be making such estimates, realizing, of course, the more or less flimsy foundations on which they were based. This understanding would imply that based on the nature of information available to them, they would have different degrees of confidence in their estimates, which is the same as the 'weight' he discussed in the *Treatise on Probability*.[14] Investors also tended to fall back on conventions, the essence of which was to assume that the existing state of affairs will continue indefinitely unless there were specific reasons for expecting changes. Also, they tended to look at what other people thought, this being partly institutionalized through the stock market. All of these features could imply violent changes in investment (although the reliance on conventions could also serve as a stabilizer); and this would make the situation even more uncertain.

Aside from repeating Keynes's own discussions, there has been some amount of original thinking on these issues amongst the Post Keynesians. Some of this has clarified Keynes's analysis, partly by comparing it to alternative thinking on uncertainty, and some of it has sought to extend Keynes's ideas.

In the former category, there have been comparisons with Keynes's views on probability and uncertainty with those of others. Thus Lawson (1988) has distinguished different views according to whether probability is a property of knowledge or belief or whether it is also an object of knowledge as a property of external material reality, and whether uncertainty corresponds to a situation of numerically measurable or immeasurable probability. Keynes, with his view that probability is a property of knowledge or belief and that uncertainty corresponds to a situation of numerically immeasurable probability, is contrasted with the views of subjectivists such as Savage and Friedman (who share Keynes's view on probability as a property of knowledge or belief but assume that uncertainty corresponds to a situation of measurable probability), and the proponents of the rational expectations view (who differ from Keynes on both counts). There has also been the issue as to whether Keynes's economic agents are irrational. Lawson (1985, 1987), Dow and Dow (1985), Carabelli (1988) and Hamouda and Smithin (1988b) argue that the behaviour that Keynes postulates is rational within the uncertain environment in which decision makers operate; in this environment they are not reduced to the inactivity of Buridan's Ass, but develop appropriate algorithms (relying on conventions, other people, etc., as mentioned above) to do the best they can. Hamouda and Smithin (1988b) also argue that the behaviour examined by Keynes is rational behaviour, although different from the type of rationality assumed by the rational expectations hypothesis: Keynes's economic agents are rational in the sense of acting in their own self-interest in a goal directed way, while in the rational expectations approach a subjective expectation of an economic variable must be equal to the conditional mathematical expectation of that variable given by the model, a much stronger assumption.

In the latter category, we may briefly mention the contributions of Shackle and Davidson. Shackle (1972) points to the problems associated with using numerical probability analysis as a basis for prediction, because many 'experiments' are 'crucial' in the sense that conducting the experiments will change the environment for future experiments, preventing the derivation of a frequency distribution. For example, an entrepreneur would regard his investment decision to be a crucial experiment. Shackle (1955) thus replaces the notion of probability by the notion of 'potential surprise', which is argued by him to be different from the former. The incidence of surprise makes individuals change their behaviour, and Shackle's (1972) view of the economy is a kaleidic one in which movement will create a completely new pattern. Davidson (1982–3, 1986, 1987) has tried to understand Keynes's contributions by distinguishing between ergodic and non-ergodic processes. An ergodic process is one in which

the probability distribution of the relevant variable calculated from any past realization tends to converge with the probability function governing the current events *and* with the probability function that will govern future outcomes.

If the process becomes non-ergodic and the probability distribution changes in an unknowable way, experience will not allow individuals to reduce the future to probability distributions in the manner done in the rational expectations hypothesis.

There has also been some criticism of Keynes's conception of probability and uncertainty, most notably by Coddington (1983). He writes:

[w]hat is unsatisfactory about focusing on the 'uncertainty' of expectations is its way of seeing knowledge and beliefs as falling so far short of some ideal state of certainty. If 'certainty' is interpreted in a way that makes it unattainable, why should we be interested in the lack of it? (Coddington, 1983, p. 55)

He goes on to argue that certainty is an ambiguous idea. He thinks it best to define it as 'a state of complete confidence in a belief together with the correctness of this belief'. But

as soon as it is admitted that any *reasonable* conception of correct foresight must allow for some (reasonable) margins of error, we are on the beginning of a slippery slope. For then we have to admit that there is no clear dichotomy between certainty and uncertainty (or between knowledge and ignorance, for that matter). Just to emphasize this point, we could go to the other extreme and claim that all foresight is 'correct' (to some sufficiently lax standards of approximation), just as all foresight is 'incorrect' (by the absurd standards of comprehensive exactness). (Coddington, 1983, p. 57)

Keynes and the Post Keynesians are, in this interpretation, requiring these absurd standards. By doing so, they have driven a wedge between behaviour and circumstance (more of this below), which involves 'analytical nihilism' or 'analytical opportunism'. This appears to us to be an unfair reading of the position of Keynes and the Post Keynesians, who have tried carefully to distinguish between situations in which foresight may be 'correct' (in situations of risk) and in which they may be 'incorrect' (true uncertainty), and have tried to analyse rational behaviour under uncertainty [see, for example, Hamouda and Smithin (1988b)]. Lawson (1987) also clarified Keynes's position and has shown how it does not necessarily lead to falling down Coddington's 'slippery slope'. He does this by distinguishing between relative knowledge and absolute knowledge: some types of knowledge, because it depends on the experience, training, etc., of the individual, is relative (consistent with empiricism), while other types of knowledge may be absolute (more in line with rationalism which gives a primary role to *a priori* reasoning in knowledge). Thus,

beliefs held as true, as knowledge, are not pure truth from an absolute standpoint, never to be replaced by a closer or better 'approximation' to reality; but neither are they sheer error. Rather they represent the best account available in terms of both logical coherence and correspondence with evidence and experience. (Lawson, 1987, pp. 962–3)

This type of dichotomy supports Lawson's (1985) earlier analysis of societal interactionism, in which individual behaviour and social structures and context are equally relevant for analysis, and of his discussion of abrupt changes in conventions during 'structural breaks' when there are qualitative changes in the structure of the economy.

The Keynesian and Post Keynesian arguments regarding uncertainty appear to us to be extremely persuasive. There is no question that there is much economic decision making which involves future possibilities to which objective probabilities just cannot be assigned. 'Experiments' are not repeated under the same conditions to allow actuarial calculations to be made. The economic environment may well be looked upon by economic agents as organic or non-ergodic, in which they make crucial experiments.

The relevant question, however, is what this implies about the behaviour of economic agents and about the behaviour of the economy. Keynes and the Post Keynesians argue that the implications are (1) that investing firms would be affected by uncertainty and not necessarily wish to invest the full employment level of saving and (2) inherent instability (which in turn would of course affect confidence).

Regarding unemployment, the strength of the argument should be obvious. If firms had full knowledge of the future (or risk could be reduced to actuarial calculations), there would be no reason for them not to invest the entire full employment level of saving in the economy. In the face of uncertainty, however, firms may not want to invest the full employment level of saving. However, it can be argued – as some of Keynes's contemporaries did – that although there could be pessimism and reduced investment due to that, full employment output would still be produced since if unemployment existed, wages would fall to induce firms to hire more labour, and if investment fell short of saving the interest rate would fall to bring saving and investment to equality at full employment. Keynes had answers to both questions: a fall in wages would not necessarily increase labour hiring since it could further increase uncertainty in the economy and otherwise reduce aggregate demand; further, since income would fall to bring saving and investment to equality, there would be no reason for the interest rate to decline, and even if the interest rate did decline, it need not affect saving and investment in the necessary directions.[15]

Regarding instability, the argument is that the existence of uncertainty (as opposed to risk) makes economic agents have at best subjective probability distributions about the unknown outcome of events, and also different degrees of confidence with which they believe such distributions. Small changes in their present environment could drastically change such degrees of confidence, and thus alter behaviour substantially, making the economy inherently unstable. This argument may not seem completely persuasive, however, even if we accept the notion of uncertainty. In the presence of such pervasive uncertainty individual agents might find some peace in the rule of thumb of following a stable behaviour when conditions change to a small degree, and only revise their actions for large changes, so that for small changes (which could be quite large in principle) in the external environment the economy would be quite stable. Heiner (1983, 1985–6), additionally, argues that a competence–difficulty gap on the part of economic agents may persuade agents to maintain their current behaviour because the likely consequences of a change in their behaviour are themselves uncertain. But the argument in favour of instability could continue further. External changes which are quite small (on average) may be large enough for some agents which could alter their behaviour, and this could change the environment for others (creating a 'structural break' as discussed above), and cumulatively create a great deal of uncertainty.[16] Even without changing the environment for others, news of changes could induce others to follow the lead of those changing their behaviour; it may make more sense to follow the crowd than to maintain one's current behaviour when others are changing theirs.

There have been some attacks on the instability argument which appear to us to be quite illegitimate. Thus Coddington (1983) has argued that investment (and asset holding) behaviour could exhibit erratic fluctuations if '(1) present conditions change erratically leading to erratically fluctuating beliefs about future circumstance; or (2) beliefs change erratically without corresponding changes in their basis in conditions'. He believes that instability of the type the Post Keynesians (and Keynes) discuss must have its origins in the second of the two, since if they were due to the first, they would not truly be autonomous, since the objective circumstances should have counterparts elsewhere in the model. Coddington thus argues that instability must insist on a subjectivist wedge between behaviour and circumstance. But once such subjectivism is introduced, the question arises as to why it should be introduced selectively (in private investment and asset holding behaviour and not in consumption and government expenditure) as done in Keynes which, according to Coddington, is crucial to Keynes's argument; further, by divorcing behaviour from circumstance, the way is opened for 'anything goes'. First, Coddington is wrong to insist that instability can only be due to changes in behaviour and not in circumstance. As already implicit in the previous paragraph, changes in confidence can be caused by changes in external circumstances. These external circumstances do not have to be variables in the model, since some of them can be implicit parameters of the model, and this follows from the use of a particular type of a dichotomy, something Coddington – in view of his insightful examination of the nature of analytical dichotomies – certainly ought to have understood. There are legitimate reasons for leaving these 'circumstances' as parameters: some could be political and truly exogenous to the model; others could be insignificant for the economy but important for some individuals; further, the relationship between these circumstances and behaviour is not stable but affected by psychological forces of which economists – as well as psychologists! – may have little definite understanding. Yet we are entitled to have some informal understanding of these issues. With no wedge necessarily introduced between behaviour and circumstance, everything does not become permissible.[17] The question regarding the selective introduction of uncertainty is a separate one, but is again both unfair and irrelevant. It is unfair because Keynes and the Post Keynesians have argued convincingly that investment and asset holding involve decision making which has future profitability considerations far greater than does consumption spending; while instability in government spending could exist, it is not for the same reasons as those that govern expectations regarding future profitability and inherent in the operation of the private enterprise system. It is irrelevant because all Keynes needs is to introduce uncertainty somewhere. If it is everywhere, the instability in the economy becomes very great (and even the value of the multiplier becomes unstable); the logical demonstration of the existence of instability is not refuted.

THE ROLE OF MONEY IN POST KEYNESIAN ECONOMICS

Post Keynesians believe that Keynes emphasized the fact that actual economies are monetary economies, rather than barter economies. The issue of money is connected closely to concepts of historical time and uncertainty. The institution of money can be thought of as a response to uncertainty, as a way of postponing the making of actual decisions; without uncertainty there would be no need to hold money except for normal transactions purposes. Money also provides an anchor to which the terms of future payments could be fixed to reduce uncertainty. But by reducing uncertainty, money also creates it: the fact that most contracts are denominated in money terms, and the fact that in modern societies money is created by uncontrolled private businesses, could be responsible for this. The existence of money is also at the root of unemployment due to the lack of demand. In the absence of money agents will supply goods only to demand others, so that Say's law will hold. Also, the payment of wages in the form of money means that firms cannot pay workers with the goods they produce, and thus resolve the effective demand problem. Neo-classical theory, by starting its analysis with barter economies, and then introducing money in a manner which is as good as not introducing it, thus misses the whole point of the Keynesian revolution which sought to integrate the monetary and real sides of economies, and provides an inadequate analysis of the macroeconomic behaviour of actual economies.

The basic thrust of these assertions is generally valid, and also generally accepted. That money is not adequately considered in general equilibrium theory, and that its incorporation in a proper way would cause enormous problems for it is candidly admitted by at least one of its ablest practitioners, Hahn. The problem, however, is that Post Keynesians sometimes argue further than they need to.

Post Keynesians have often made the claim that in an economy without money there could be no unemployment, so that the essence of the Keynesian revolution is the proper analysis of money. One argument, as noted above, is that otherwise firms would pay workers not in terms of money but in terms of their product, automatically creating a demand for their products. This argument is not persuasive in a multi-commodity world in which consumer-workers are not specialized in consumption and insist on wage payment in product bundles. Also firms would realize that the offer of employment does not imply the automatic creation of demand for its product and the problem of effective demand would arise. The other argument is that an asset such as money is required to drive a wedge between income and spending: individuals can hold money which can be produced without generating employment. Some writers, such as Drazen (1980), have argued that money is not required to divorce income from current spending; the existence of any non-produced asset will do the same. While this is true for an individual, it is not true in the aggregate, since the purchase of such an asset by one individual would put purchasing power into the sellers' hands, which could be spent on employment-generating goods. Thus money seems to be necessary for an overall discrepancy between (full-employment) income and spending, which would result in unemployment. However, it is not enough to show that money is necessary for unemployment. It must be shown that in a monetary economy unemployment is possible (sufficiency need not be insisted upon since Keynes did not deny that a monetary economy could sometimes be at full employment).

Suppose instead of spending on goods individuals want to hold money, which pushes up the price of money and asset demand spills over into other assets, the production of which (and hence employment generation) will be stimulated. Here Davidson (1972, 1980) invokes the essential properties of money: zero elasticity of output and employment, so that in the face of increasing demand for it more money cannot either be produced, or can be produced without increasing more employment (thereby taking the economy to full employment); and zero substitutability with other assets, which prevents substitution from money to other assets, presumably because of the unique characteristic of liquidity possessed by money. Here we must agree with Friedman (1974) that Davidson

appears to *start* from the proposition that there does not exist a long run equilibrium position characterized by full employment, and then try to *deduce* the empirical characteristics of money (and other elements of the economy) from that proposition.

This does not show that the existence of something empirical called money implies unemployment; it merely gives a definition of what property money must have if its existence is to result in unemployment. Such a money need not exist in the real world. However, by relying on only these two essential properties of money, Davidson is doing himself an injustice. The other institutional consequences which he and other Post Keynesians discuss – such as uncertainty, contracts in money terms, and the endogeneity of money supply, together with limited substitutability – may well be enough to imply unemployment in the economy. We consider these issues in turn.

As mentioned above, Post Keynesians view the holding of money to be, at least in part, a way of postponing the making of irreversible decisions in an uncertain environment. They argue that this way (which is the correct way) of perceiving money implies changing the whole basis of the theory of the interest rate. The classical economists had believed in the notion of the natural rate of interest, which is determined in the market for loans by the intersection of a downward-sloping investment schedule and an upward-rising savings schedule (as discussed in chapter 2). Keynes's theory however, it is argued, made the interest rate a monetary phenomenon in the sense it was determined by the supply and demand for money. The demand for money would depend on the rate of interest, but would not be a stable function of it since its position would depend on the normal rate of interest.[18] This normal rate was the one expected by individuals, and was thus determined by the state of expectations about asset prices; these expectations could change over time, particularly when there were changes in the economic environment facing asset-holders. Tobin (1958) had ignored all these issues by assuming away uncertainty and considering only risk. The supply of money was assumed by Keynes to be given. The implication of all this was that in the Post Keynesian analysis the rate of interest becomes a monetary phenomenon which is strongly affected by expectations; it would thus not be able to play the role of equilibrating saving and investment in the market of loanable funds, to ensure that the full employment level of output could be sold, as required in classical theory.

A second important idea regarding money in Post Keynesian thinking is that it served as a tool with which to reduce the
amount of uncertainty in the economy. By being something in
terms of which contracts could be made, it could serve to
introduce some stability into the economy. This aspect has
been stressed by Lerner (1952), Davidson (1972) and Wells
(1978, 1979b). The most important of such contracts is the
money wage contract, since as Wells (1979b) writes:

[i]n view of the universal use of labor, it follows that the cost of labor plays a
dominant role in determining the overall level of costs of production and
hence prices of any modern money using production–exchange economy.
Other things being equal, every rise or fall in the money wage rate will
produce a responding rise or fall in all costs and in all prices. (Wells, 1979b,
p. 394)

The money wage rate . . . is the *numeraire* of the monetary system, and to
have a stable *numeraire*, sticky money wages are essential. Sticky wage rates
imply sticky costs of production and a relatively stable value of money. With
these conditions holding, economic plans can be drawn up, wage and other
contracts specified in money terms, costs calculated. (Wells, 1979b, p. 398)

The implication is that individual entrepreneurs would try to
fix money wages by entering into long-term contracts in order
to reduce uncertainty in their own operations. But the unin-
tended consequence of this is to stabilize the entire economy.
If money wages were made flexible, the economy would be
subject to wild gyrations in the wage and the price.

A third important strand in the writing of many Post
Keynesians is that money supply is endogenous. They have
generally argued that instead of taking the supply of money to
be vertical, it is more sensible to take it to be horizontal. Many
reasons for this have been suggested. First, if money is defined
in a way which includes those assets which satisfy the two
essential properties of money, and if these properties (at least
the zero elasticity of substitution property) are subjective, the
supply of money may vary with changes in people's perceptions as to what satisfies these definitions. Another way of
stating this would be to say that given a particular empirical
definition of money, there would be changes in the velocity of
money (although there could be other reasons for changes in
velocity as well). Second, and what has received much more

attention in the Post Keynesian literature, money in the actual world is essentially credit money, and not commodity money. As long as banks are willing to lend to firms at a given lending rate, the supply of money, as a result of changes in the stock of bank loans, will vary with the monetary needs of firms for working capital (which would depend on production levels) and fixed capital (which would depend on the level of investment).[19] It is important to note that the money supply rises *and* falls with increases and decreases in demand. Increases occur due to the creation of new loans, while decreases can occur due to the repayment of existing loans. This view of money creation is sharply contrasted with the mainstream approach to the endogeneity of money, according to which the supply of money is determined by the stock of money and the money multiplier, which depends on the reserve–deposit ratio chosen by banks and the currency–deposit ratio chosen by the public. The Post Keynesians argue that banks do not choose a reserve–deposit ratio but allow it to change according to the demand for loans. It may be argued that this view overlooks the fact that banks may be reserve constrained, and so may not be able to meet all loan demand. This criticism, Post Keynesians argue, does not take into account the institutional facts of the banking system. Banks have many means at their disposal to attract more currency into the banking system. They can issue new types of certificates of deposit or new types of deposit accounts; they can allow customers to make use of overdraft facilities (this is particularly the case in France) and then try to obtain reserves by looking for currency after making loans (although the reserve requirements do not have to be met all the time); and finally they can turn to the Central Bank's discount window. Rousseas (1986) has developed a Kaleckian theory of markup pricing by these banks: they are assumed to hold excess reserves, fix the interest rate as a markup on the discount rate, and adjust loans in line with demand; this is one of the rare attempts to model banking behaviour to explain a horizontal supply curve for money. Third, Post Keynesians have argued that Central Banks tend to supply money to meet the level required by economic activity, at a fixed interest rate.[20] This is because their primary obligation is to ensure the liquidity of the financial system and to provide lender-of-last resort facilities. Thus, it is observed that even if the money multiplier is shown to be roughly stable, it does not show that the direction of causation is from base money to money stock; empirical studies have sought to show that the causality is the other way around.[21] Of course, the Central Bank can seek to control the money supply, but this it can do effectively only by changing the interest rate at which it will make reserves available. As a result of all this, the supply of money schedule is viewed as being horizontal rather than vertical.

Some criticisms have been raised regarding this perspective. Minsky (1982) has argued that money supply can expand due to credit expansion not just for production and investment purposes but also for speculation and for the expansion of conglomerates. The expansion of this non-productive credit can eventually lead to a credit crunch when banks refuse to extend additional finance due to a failure in their confidence. However, Minsky's discussions of a crisis situation, in which firms can go bankrupt and thus reduce the amount of money, can be interpreted as supportive of the endogeneity of money idea (see below). A middle position – between the vertical and horizontal supply curves – can also be argued,[22] on the basis of some type of behaviour pattern of commercial banks which takes into account their desires to control their asset structures rather than becoming completely passive. Finally, even the agenda of Central Banks can be questioned. Experience in the US and UK can be interpreted as reflecting that the Central Banks may occasionally step on the brakes. Indeed, not all Post Keynesians believe that money supply is completely endogenous (that is, completely horizontal). Nor, as we shall see later, do they need to for showing the persistence of unemployment.

Keynes himself, in the *General Theory*, seems to be assuming a given supply of money, but this does not imply that he believed this to be the actual state of affairs; moreover in chapter 12 (p. 158) he comments on the role of banks in affecting investment and in chapter 19 (p. 266) explicitly mentions this possibility. In his 1937 paper on the interest rate, by talking of the finance motive, Keynes made it easier to develop an endogenous theory of money from his work,[23] and in a later 1937 *Economic Journal* paper again stresses the role of bank credit in the transition from a higher to lower level of activity.[24]

There is one anomaly, however. If for Keynes an essential property of money was zero elasticity of production, how is this consistent with *any* endogeneity of money supply? Dow (1985, p. 187) justifies the need for this property by arguing that if money is to be held, it must be able to retain its value relative to goods; but if money 'were in elastic supply, then its value would be eroded if an increase in demand always called forth an increase in supply'. The problem with this view is that increasing the supply of money will not necessarily, under Keynesian conditions, increase the price level. Keynes's property had to do more with the zero elasticity of employment: for, otherwise, a rise in demand for money would increase employment and take the economy to full employment.

In addition to all this discussion, there has been some new interest in trying to elaborate on Keynes's discussion of a 'liquidity-premium' on account of the 'potential convenience or security' it affords to the holder [JMK, VII, p. 226], related to the two essential properties of money, especially the second, the elasticity of substitution. Bhattacharjea (1987) writes that, unlike other assets, money is not subject to 'moral' risk, taxes and carrying costs; it is of special importance because contracts are denominated in terms of money and it has zero transactions costs; this makes the 'marginal efficiency' of money balances, the interest rate, have some floor. And this nominal interest 'rules the roost'. Kregel (1983b) and Nell (1983) have examined how Keynes's approach drew on Sraffa's (1932) critique of Hayek's *Prices and Production*, in showing how in equilibrium the rates of return (depending on the spot and future prices) of durable commodities were equalized with the money rate of interest due to arbitrage. Thus the money rate of interest determined the other rates of return.[25] The Wicksellian analysis in which the natural rate of interest was determined by the real forces of productivity and thrift (and the actual rate could be pushed away – in a disequilibrium situation – from it when banks created or destroyed money), was replaced by Keynes's showing that the interest rate was determined by the yield on money, and the real rates adjusted to it, thereby properly integrating the real and monetary aspects of the economy. The real rates could thus not play the role of adjusting investment to full employment saving.

EQUILIBRIUM AND POST KEYNESIAN ECONOMICS

Finally, Post Keynesians believe that the analytical concept of equilibrium – so central to neo-classical theory – is not a useful device, and in fact inconsistent with a proper analysis of monetary economies in which uncertainty prevails and which is travelling along historical time. Such economies are inherently unstable (due to sudden shifts in the level of investment, reflecting sudden shifts in the state of long-term expectations, as discussed above) rather than being in, or tending towards, a tranquil state of equilibrium.

There are actually two different issues here: first, whether the economy is inherently unstable, and second, whether it is appropriate to use the tool of equilibrium. We have already examined the first question; let us turn to the second.

To do so, one must distinguish between two different notions of equilibrium. First, there is the restricted neo-classical notion in which all markets are assumed to clear. Since in this notion even the labour market must clear, it would appear that there would be no room for unemployment; thus this notion of equilibrium is incompatible with Keynes's analysis. There *are* ways of reconciling the two notions, market clearing equilibrium and involuntary unemployment. Darity and Horn (1983) have tried to do so by defining (following one of Keynes's definitions) involuntary unemployment as a situation in which an increase in aggregate demand is associated with an increase in output and making the supply of labour depend on wealth. Then, even with labour-market clearing, an increase in aggregate demand will affect the real wealth, shift the labour supply curve and increase the level of employment. However, this notion of involuntary unemployment is not one which many Post Keynesians – or other Keynesians, for that matter – would find satisfying since it goes against the idea that unemployment refers to a situation when workers are looking for jobs but unable to find them.[26] More generally, because of other assumptions which are introduced into the neo-classical general equilibrium analysis, Post Keynesians have been hostile to this notion.[27]

But to reject the neo-classical notion is not to reject the notion of equilibrium itself. A second notion of equilibrium, in which given the values of some exogenous variables (the choice of these will depend on the question at hand and need not always be the same), the system being considered comes to a position of rest. Post Keynesians seem often to have trouble with this more general notion of unemployment. Rotheim (1988), for example, writes that a 'metaphysical system based on the principle of equilibrium simply has no room for the concept of uncertainty or the discourse that emanates from this concept'. We have already cited Shackle's (1982) thoughts on the matter. Hicks (1976) has gone so far as to criticize Keynes's own method of equilibrium analysis, claiming that it does not consider the movement of the economy over historical time.

Even if we believe that the economy is inherently unstable, this does not imply that we must reject equilibrium analysis (in the more general sense). In rejecting neo-classical general equilibrium analysis the Post Keynesians have had a tendency to throw the baby out with the bathwater.[28] The notion of equilibrium – cleansed of neo-classical influences – simply says that we specify a set of parameters and fix their values, and solve for the equilibrium values of the variables.[29] There is no reason to insist that the economy is actually at that equilibrium, but close to it, and having a tendency to go towards it. Even if the economy is always at the equilibrium, the economy is not necessarily in a tranquil state since the parameters held constant in defining the equilibrium can be changing all the time, perhaps according to some laws of motion which can be studied in a more inclusive model, or perhaps in a way that may defy formal analysis. A valid criticism of a particular equilibrium theory (for example the neo-classical one) may be that it does not consider the instability of some parameters due to reasons such as uncertainty, so that it is led to incorrect specifications of individual behaviour in equilibrium, but it does not follow that the notion of equilibrium must be jettisoned.[30]

As mentioned above, there is one sense in which Post Keynesians may have legitimate worries about the equilibrium method, and this is when the position of the equilibrium depends on the path through which the economy reaches the equilibrium. This notion seems to highlight the role of history in economic analysis. In this case the analysis of the equilibrium position, without any analysis of the path, may be seriously misleading. This problem, however, also does not imply that the equilibrium method must be given up. First, the economy, in its movement along the path can be analysed as a moving equilibrium, so that examination of the path does not imply the abandonment of the equilibrium method in the sense defined above. Second, Post Keynesians have not provided many examples of why – at least in short-run analysis of the type with which we are concerned here[31] – the final equilibrium may be path-dependent. One possible example can be constructed from what Kregel (1976) calls the shifting equilibrium model. In this model, long-period expectations may be affected by the disappointment of short-period expectations. If this dependence can be represented by a simple functional relationship between the long- and short-period expectations, no path dependence will arise. If, however, long-period expectation is a function of some weighted average (with perhaps variable weights) of short-period expectations, we may obtain path dependence. But Post Keynesians have not argued that this type of relationship between the two types of expectations actually holds.[32]

The rejection of equilibrium analysis of all types implies the rejection of formal modelling.[33] While there is certainly much room for what Shackle (1984) calls 'rhetorical' work in economics, as opposed to 'axiomatic' work, there is the danger both of internal obscurity and of the breakdown of communication with economists of other varieties. With mainstream neo-classical economics – rightly or wrongly – having made technical formalism part of its methodological morality,[34] there is a danger of Post Keynesian economics being largely ignored by the economics profession. Solow (1979) in his partial review of alternative approaches to macroeconomic theory passes the following unfavourable judgement:[35]

Some of the post-Keynesians seem to regard . . . [the] emphasis on dynamics, on the instability or at least non-stability of an unmanaged capitalist economy, as the essence of the doctrine. But I cannot see how to associate this view with the rather violent attacks on the North American style of model-building that usually accompany it. One would think that instability or non-stability would be a likely candidate for model-building. The proper way to do macroeconomics can hardly be *all* historical context and *no* analytical structure. Unfortunately the school has provided no systematic description or example of what it conceives to be the right way to do macroeconomic theory. Thus far so-called post-Keynesianism seems to be more a state of mind than a theory.

Keynes, despite drawing only one diagram in the *General Theory*, and despite his footnote (JMK, VII, p. 280) stating 'those who (rightly) dislike algebra will lose little by omitting the first section of this chapter', does write down a few equations in the *General Theory*,[36] and discusses in modelling language (although verbally) his analysis in several places, most notably in chapter 18. He also proceeds to show how unemployment can exist within the analytical framework of those that he called the classical economists. Indeed, as we have argued in chapter 3, he does have an 'equilibrium' model in the *General Theory*.

THE AGGREGATE DEMAND – AGGREGATE SUPPLY MODEL

It is not quite fair to say, however, that the Post Keynesians have not developed formal models to represent their views on the functioning of the economy and criticisms of alternative

models. They have developed, usually in a manner faithful to
Keynes's (JMK, VII) chapter 3 analysis, the aggregate demand
and aggregate supply diagram which plots the level of employment on the horizontal axis and money values (the product of
prices and quantities) on the vertical. Keynes did not rigor-
ously develop this model, leaving the derivation of the curves
vague; Post Keynesians have tried to formalize it to show the
determination of equilibrium in the short period, and also to
examine the process of dynamics to that equilibrium, following Keynes's analysis of chapter 5. Several derivations of the
model are available,[37] though not all are internally quite
consistent. We provide a brief description of a logically
consistent representation,[38] and point out some problems with
some other approaches. Post Keynesians, partly on the basis
of their acceptance of this model, have criticized other 'Keynesian' models. We will also examine the nature of these criticisms and briefly evaluate them.

Assume that firms are perfectly competitive in the sense of
producing a homogeneous product as atomistic agents. However, they do not have perfect knowledge regarding the future.
They have to make production plans before knowing what
price they will receive upon selling it; we assume that they
make a point estimate of the price, which reflects their short-
term expectations, along the lines discussed in chapter 3.
They also have to invest in order to produce in the more distant
future, and such decisions are governed by their long-term
expectations. Assume that given long-term expectations,
firms plan to invest a given amount in real terms. There are
two income classes: workers who receive a fixed money wage
and consume all their income, and capitalists who receive
profits and consume a fixed amount in real terms.[39] The firms
are identical so that we can use the device of the representative
firm.

In Keynes's 'day', or Marshall's market period, firms have
a given expected price and produce to maximize expected
profits. The level of employment in the economy is shown by
the intersection of the aggregate supply (Z) curve and the
expected proceeds (E) curve in Figure 5.1. The Z curve,

showing the profit maximizing level of the value of output at any level of employment, is given by

$$Z(N) = W F(N)/F'(N) \qquad (5.1)$$

with given W, the money wage,[40] and the E curve, showing the value of output at any given level of employment for a particular expected price, is given by[41]

$$E(N) = P^e F(N) \qquad (5.2)$$

for a given expected price P^e, where N is the level of employment, and F(N) the production function (given the level of capital). Both curves are obviously upward rising and the Z curve steeper than the E curve. Note that at the point of intersection we have

$$W/P^e = F'(N) \qquad (5.3)$$

which implies profit maximization at the given expected price. There is no reason, however, why the price expectation will be realized, so that expected proceeds will equal actual proceeds. In the market period, given the output and employment chosen by firms the product price, P, will adjust to clear the market and equate aggregate demand to output. Given our assumptions, and denoting the real level of investment and capitalist consumption by I, the equilibrium is given by

$$F(N) = WN/P + I \qquad (5.4)$$

so that the market period equilibrium price is

$$P = WN/[F(N) - I] \qquad (5.5)$$

We can thus draw the actual proceeds curve A, showing the relationship between the actual value of output realized by the firm in the market at any level of employment, given by

$$A(N) = WNF(N)/[F(N) - I] \qquad (5.6)$$

Depending on whether the expected price is higher or lower than the actual price, $E(N) >$ or $< A(N)$ at any N.

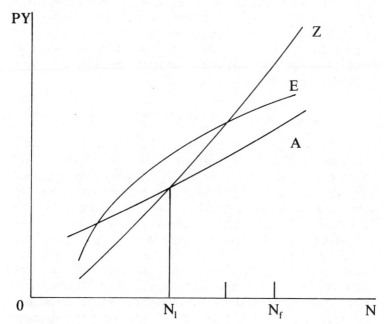

Figure 5.1

Beyond the 'day' the firm, if its price expectation is not realized, revises its expectation. Assume that if $P^e > P$ the firm revises its P^e down (but not all the way down to P) and conversely for the opposite case. In the short run this will imply a series of shifting market period equilibria with the E curve moving (up if P^e is increased and down if it is reduced). In short-run equilibrium, the firm's price expectation must be fulfilled so that it will not wish to change its level of employment, so that the E curve must have shifted to intersect the Z and A curves at their point of intersection. Notice that there is no reason why the short-run equilibrium level of employment is at full employment, since it depends on the parameters of the Z and A curves, and in the figure the short-run equilibrium level of employment, N_1, is shown to be less than the full employment level N_f, which can be taken to be given by the level of employment at which the marginal product for labour is equal to the marginal disutility of work. Note also that if there is a fall in the level of the money wage in response to unemployment, the Z and A curves will shift down by the same vertical amount, leaving the short-run equilibrium level of employment unchanged, and given (from equations (5.1) and (5.6)) by

$$N = G(I) \quad G' > 0 \tag{5.7}$$

where $G^{-1} = F(N) - NF'(N)$.

Those who have tried to develop Keynes's chapter 3 model (since Keynes did not examine it in a rigorous manner), however, have not always done so in an internally consistent manner, and this can be seen by comparing their efforts to our formulation. The problems generally have to do with the derivation of what we have called the expected proceeds and actual proceeds curves. Keynes did not actually have such functions and curves; instead he had what he called the aggregate demand function which apparently depended on the consumption and investment behaviour in the economy. Weintraub (1958), Davidson and Smolensky (1964) and others have derived this curve as follows. For any level of employment, N, they find the corresponding level of output from the production function, Y, then the corresponding level of consumption and investment in real terms, and value it at the price consistent with profit-maximization at the given wage W, that is, $P = W/F'(N)$. In terms of the simple model we have been using, this implies an aggregate demand function,[42] $D(N)$ given by

$$D(N) = WN + [W/F'(N)]I \tag{5.8}$$

Drawing this curve in the same diagram as the aggregate demand curve Z(N), they argue that for any given level of employment D(N) shows the value of demand and Z(N) the value of supply; excess demand (supply) leads to an expansion (contraction) of employment, so that equilibrium is established, for the given W at the point where $Z(N) = D(N)$, Keynes's point of effective demand. The problem with this view is that for a given N, actual money demand will have to be priced at the market-clearing price given by (5.5) and not by $W/F'(N)$, which is equal to P^e which, except at short-period equilibrium, is not equal to the P.[43] Regarding the expected proceeds curve, Post Keynesians have used it to show the adjustment to short-period equilibrium, but many of them run into problems regarding it. Wells (1962) assumes in a competitive model that expected price will fall with the level of employment, so that his curve is concave both for this reason and for diminishing returns; the problem with this is that perfectly competitive firms must take the expected price as given.[44] Wells (1978) suggests that his expected proceeds function has a positive slope to reflect the fact that firms believe that higher employment will make for more robust markets; this cannot happen under perfect competition because firms will assume that they can sell everything at their expected price and market prospects therefore become irrelevant. Torr (1981) and Parrinello (1980) rightly criticize this approach but go to the extreme of assuming a horizontal expected sales curve for a given state of expectations; this again is inconsistent with perfect competition where firms must expect a given price not a given value of sales. Our expected proceeds curve follows Casarosa's (1981).

The model developed here has assumed perfect competition, which was the assumption that Keynes made in the *General Theory*, since he accepted the classical postulate of the real wage being equal to the marginal product of labour. Post Keynesians generally argue that Keynes did this to show how unemployment could occur in a framework that was as close as possible to the mainstream approach of his day, which assumed perfect competition [see Kregel (1987)]. Post Keynesians have used alternative assumptions about market structure to develop models of the type just considered, going closer to Keynes's (JMK, VII, p. 245) more general assumption of a 'given . . . degree of competition'. Thus Tarshis (1979) and Chick (1983, chapter V) have replaced perfect competition by monopoly, while Weintraub (1958), for instance, has developed a markup pricing model, making it more like Kalecki's (1971) model. Ball (1964), Wood (1975), Eichner (1976), and Harcourt and Kenyon (1976), among others, have extended this approach to relate the pricing policies of firms (that is, the level of the markup) to the financial needs for accumulation.

The Post Keynesians have used models of this type to criticize those who do Keynesian economics with the income–expenditure model (45° diagram model and its successive developments, including the IS–LM), identifying them as 'bastard Keynesians'. Among other things, they argue that

1. the level of output is determined by the interaction of demand (consumption, investment) and supply (technology, wages) and not by demand alone as in the diagonal cross model;
2. the price level is a variable in the short run, and not fixed, as in the IS–LM model (or in the claims made by Leijonhufvud (1969));[45] this and other problems make the model fundamentally contradictory with Keynes's analysis;
3. that since the Z and A curves intersect to determine the level of N, the demand for labour depends on the demand for goods and is not given by the marginal product curve, as in the models of the 'bastard' Keynesians; and
4. wage rigidity does not cause unemployment as claimed by bastard Keynesians, since even with money wage reductions in their (the Post Keynesian) model, unemployment does not disappear.

While the Post Keynesian model presented above can be internally consistent and faithful in principle to Keynes's discussion in chapters 3 and 5, it cannot support the weight of all the criticisms of other approaches made on its basis. It does show, of course, that Keynes – as opposed to many other Keynesians and Kalecki – did not assume a fixed price level (as in the textbook IS–LM model) and his revolution was not concerned with reversing the speeds of price and quantity adjustment as initially claimed by Leijonhufvud.[46] If the diagonal cross model is in error, it is so only in assuming that aggregate demand is independent of changes in monetary variables (which legitimately allows it to determine the short-run equilibrium value of output by considering only the demand side); it does not necessarily assume fixed prices,[47] although countless textbook discussions do make this assumption and seem to be following Kalecki's rather than Keynes's analysis.

Because it illustrates some important issues, we consider in some more detail the controversy surrounding the IS–LM model, Pasinetti (1974) has argued that Keynes's method was to use a system of causal equations: in his system the demand for, and supply of, money determined the interest rate, the interest rate and long-period expectations determined investment and investment and the consumption function determined output and employment; the simultaneity of the IS–LM model destroys this whole causal chain. He writes that

what inevitably happens is that, behind the formal *facade* of a simultaneous equation system, a substitution of interpretive models takes place. The typical features of an industrial society are made to recede and the character-istic features of a rather imaginary 'exchange' economy are imperceptibly slipped in instead. Within such a context, it is not surprising that what is said by Keynes becomes more or less irrelevant, or can only appear as referring to 'imperfections' of the market, 'rigidities' of prices and wages or 'liquidity traps'. (Pasinetti, 1974, pp. 47–8)

The IS–LM model, in fact, is a favourite whipping-dog of Post Keynesians,[48] because it has given rise to the 'rigidity' and 'imperfection' interpretations of Keynes.[49] Hicks (1976, 1980–81) has spoken out against his own creation, writing that the diagram 'is now much less popular with me than I think it is still with many other people' (Hicks, 1976). Hicks (1980–81) raises problems concerning the stock-flow equilibrium nature of the model which creates problems both for the analysis of comparative statics changes during the short run and conse-quently for policy analysis, and regarding the failure of the model to take expectations seriously so as to allow for liquidity preference in equilibrium. However, some facts in support of the IS–LM method can also be marshalled. First, Keynes himself seems to have endorsed the approach when he wrote of Hicks's formalization: 'I found it very interesting, and really have next to nothing to say by way of criticism' [JMK, XIV, p. 79]. Second, as Young (1987) has shown, the IS–LM model is not a quirky creation of Hicks, but similar expositions were developed by several others, including Reddaway, Harrod and Meade; this may be taken to suggest that Keynes's analysis appeared to be similar to the IS–LM approach to several people (although because they were often in close contact, it cannot strongly be argued that this feeling was arrived at independently). Third, the majority of Keynesian economists have come to accept IS–LM as *the* Keynesian model of the economy.[50] While this in itself is not a convincing argument, particularly because this book takes the view that the majority of macroeconomists have diverted attention away from very important matters in Keynesian economics, strong and spirited defences of the model have been produced. Solow (1984), for example, argues that the model's equilibrium can be seen as a point in a dynamic process, where changes in flows affect the stocks in the next 'period', and that this is a correct way of integrating stocks and flows. However, he is not entirely convincing because he fails to take into account the problems raised by a Keynesian notion of uncertainty.

Our own interpretation supports an intermediate position, where the IS–LM approach (with the wage given, not the price) can be taken to be a version of the equilibrium model in the *General Theory*, though somewhat different from what we have called Keynes's equilibrium model in chapter 3 since it takes the feedback effect of income on the demand for money into account. However, since it does not explicitly take into account expectations, uncertainty, historical time and money, it cannot be thought of as a complete depiction of Keynes's system which, we have argued in chapter 3, also had market-period and historical models. As Hicks (1982, p. 100) himself was to write later of his creation, 'it is no more than a part of what Keynes was saying, or implying, that can be represented in that manner, and it was easy to take it as the whole'. In our judgement, the Post Keynesians have been too critical of the IS–LM model because it ignores expectations, uncertainty and historical time. These criticisms give Keynes's endorsement of the model more significance than it deserves. The model – as even Hicks states – should be thought of as formalizing only a part of Keynes's analysis, namely that which analyses the determination of short-run equilibrium. There need be nothing wrong in confining attention to that part if it is remembered that it is not the whole. In particular, it should be remembered that the short-run equilibrium is a point in history linked to an irreversible past and an uncertain future. Moreover, the model should not be used for purposes for which it was not intended. In particular, since it is an incomplete picture of Keynes's analysis, it cannot be used to explore what is the crucial feature of the Keynesian revolution. It is this illegitimate use of the model that led – at least in part – to the development of the rigidities and imperfections views that so worried Pasinetti and others. Recognition of the dynamic arguments is essential for understanding the complete Keynesian system, with appropriate attention to uncertainty and a variety of other influences, influences which are hidden and lost in the functional forms of the equations of the IS–LM model. However, these kinds of issues are also missing from the Post Keynesian model as presented above.

Turning next to the demand curve for labour, the criticism has been made that the standard representations of the Keynesian model show that the real wage determines the demand for labour by firms, while the Post Keynesian model shows that it is actually determined by the demand for goods. This claim has been made by, for example, Weintraub (1958), Davidson and Smolensky (1964), Davidson (1983), Mishan (1964) and E. R. Weintraub (1974). It is argued that while in perfectly competitive markets it is true that the real wage is equal to the marginal product of labour, the cause of an expansion of the demand for labour (when it occurs) is a rise in the demand for goods, not a fall in the real wage. The problem with this approach is that it confuses comparative statics properties with behavioural functions. The demand curve for labour should show what causes firms to change their behaviour regarding their plans to hire labour. Competitive firms, clearly, cannot make estimates of how much they can sell since they do not face sales constraints. Thus the labour hiring decisions of perfectly competitive firms must depend on the real wage. However, there is a grain of truth in the argument, since this decision will depend on the *expected* real wage which, except at short-period equilibrium, will not be equal to the *actual* real wage. When aggregate demand for goods increases, it will lead to more labour being hired and more output being produced, but this must be a *result* of a rise in the price and a resultant upward revision of the expected price and a fall in the expected real wage. Thus even though it is true, as the Post Keynesians claim, that aggregate demand and aggregate supply curves determine employment in short-run equilibrium, and the marginal product curve then determines the real wage, firms as price takers in perfectly competitive markets treat the expected real wage parametrically in making their employment decision.

Finally, the claim that wage flexibility does not restore full employment cannot be adequately sustained in terms of the assumptions of the model made thus far. In the neo-classical synthesis achieved by the bastard Keynesians, wage flexibility would restore full employment by the so-called Keynes effect in which a fall in the money wage would increase the real supply of money in the economy, reduce the interest rate and increase investment and the level of aggregate demand. Others have added the real balance effect [which was not mentioned by Keynes (JMK, VII)], by which the increase in the real money supply would directly stimulate spending. These monetary considerations are absent in the Post Keynesian model, since the level of investment is assumed to be constant (thus ruling out the Keynes effect) and spending does not depend on real balances (thus ruling out the real balance effect). If, for example, investment were to depend on the rate of interest, a fall in W could reduce the interest rate and raise the level of investment. This would imply that a fall in W would make the Z curve shift down more than the A curve, increasing N. (This is also obvious from equation (5.7), since I rises.) Thus the Post Keynesian position cannot be sustained in terms of the model.[51] It seems that Keynesian unemployment is possible only with money wage rigidity in the face of unemployment, and does not have much to do with historical time, uncertainty, money, or inherent instability.[52]

One remaining question remains concerning why Post Keynesians insist on using Keynes's aggregate demand–aggregate supply diagram (using money values on the vertical and employment level on the horizontal axis) rather than other versions which have become more popular in macroeconomic theory when, as we argue, it has no *intrinsic* advantages over the other presentations.[53] The Post Keynesian soft spot for the diagram is explained perhaps by the fact that it comes closest to Keynes's own formulation of the problem.[54] His reason for the departure from the standard practice of using unit price supply and demand curves had to do with the fact that with many goods one could not add up their quantities and prices while one could add up levels of employment (assuming it to be homogeneous, or expressed in efficiency units) and aggregate values. Moreover, even with one good, the existence of many firms all with their own expected price, meant that one cannot infer the point of production from a standard supply curve. It should be realized, however, that Keynes's use of his apparatus can be justified only under strong conditions: it has to be assumed that a given aggregate employment has to be distributed in a unique way between different industries and firms (see, for example, Asimakopulos, 1982). If we are willing to make such an assumption there seems to be no reason not to go all the way and assume that there is a single (representative) firm producing a single good, the single good and price assumption being justified as an approximation using price and quantity index numbers.[55] There may be an additional pedagogical reason why Keynes used employment as the adjusting variable rather than output or income. In chapter 2 of the *General Theory* he presented the classical theory in which employment was determined by the marginal product and marginal disutility schedules; his theory could be sharply contrasted to that if he showed how the level of employment was determined instead by aggregate demand and supply. But this does not imply that other formulations are incorrect.

THE IMPLICATIONS OF WAGE REDUCTIONS AND WAGE FLEXIBILITY

The problems discussed in the previous section do not imply that Post Keynesians are wrong, only that the model they usually use does not by itself make their case for them. In fact, their position can be argued forcefully in terms of the model used in chapter 2, developed by the bastard Keynesians and now proliferating macroeconomics textbooks.[56] This model uses aggregate demand and aggregate supply curves but measures real output on the horizontal axis and the unit goods price on the vertical.

The usual presentation draws a downward-sloping aggregate demand curve, AD as in Figure 2.5. To recapitulate, it is downward sloping for a closed economy because of the Keynes effect or the real balance effect. The aggregate supply curve, AS, is upward rising given the money wage; for example, for the economy described in the Post Keynesian model, it would be given by

$$P = W/F'(F^{-1}(Y)) \qquad (5.8)$$

The intersection of the AD and AS curves determines the short-run equilibrium level of Y, which could well be less than Y_f, which employs the full-employment labour force. With unemployment, W falls over time, pushing the AS curve downwards, till the short-run equilibrium level of output results in full employment. Unemployment would persist only if the money wage was rigid and prevented the economy from moving down the AD curve to a position of full employment.

This analysis implicitly assumes that the AD curve is (i) downward sloping and (ii) does not shift when the AS curve shifts. We now argue that these assumptions can be sustained only by arbitrarily ignoring a variety of factors emphasized by Keynes and/or the Post Keynesians. In the discussion we assume that the AD curve, like the AS curve representing equation (5.8), is drawn for a given money wage.

First, the level of investment may not respond positively to a fall in the interest rate, so that one reason for the downward slope of the AD curve would disappear. For a world with pervasive uncertainty, Keynes emphasized that investment decisions depended largely on expected long-term yields on capital assets, and such expectations may not be affected by reductions in interest rates (chapter 12, especially p. 164). Rather than being an unrealistic special case (of a general case which assumes that there is a presumption that investment depends on the interest rate), it may be the general case.[57] By jettisoning Keynes's approach to uncertainty and reducing it to calculable risk, Keynesians have tended to overlook the relationship between investment and uncertainty and stress the relationship between investment and the interest rate – the way to reintroduce Keynesian results was to bring in elasticity pessimism.[58]

Second, the real balance effect provides an incomplete picture of changes in the position of asset holders in the economy. Since nominal assets held by them are not just liabilities of monetary authorities (outside money), but more importantly those of other individuals, firms and banks, a fall in P would redistribute real wealth from debtors to creditors. The effect on real spending would depend on the extent of wealth redistribution and the partial derivatives of real spending with respect to real wealth: if debtors have higher marginal propensities to spend than creditors, a net reduction in real spending would follow.[59] These arguments have been made by Kalecki (1944), Leijonhufvud (1968), Wells (1979b), Davidson (1985), and Minsky (1982) (who emphasizes the debt position of firms). The argument is not made by Keynes (JMK, VII), who does not mention the real balance effect, but there is every reason to believe that he agreed with these arguments.[60]

Third, the downward-sloping AD curve assumes a given nominal supply of money, and therefore ignores the endogeneity of that supply in real economies. For example, when P falls, firms may find it harder to repay their loans from banks; many of them may default. This would result in reductions in bank assets and hence liabilities, resulting in a decline in credit money. The situation could be aggravated by a spurt of bank failures, further reducing the supply of credit money. Even without such dramatic events, banks may recall loans to firms when P begins to fall; also firms would pay back loans to banks as their demand for money fell. These possibilities have been explored in Wells (1979b), Minsky (1982) and Davidson (1982). If the reductions in nominal money supply reduce spending, the level of aggregate demand will fall.[61]

Fourth, changes in P would also result in redistributions of income if all incomes in money terms did not change proportionately with P. The effect on aggregate demand would depend on differences in marginal propensities to spend by different groups. This possibility was noted by Keynes (JMK, VII, p. 262), and developed by Post Keynesians, as in Davidson and Smolensky (1964). Joan Robinson (1937), in her long-period extension of the *General Theory*, also made different saving propensities of interest earning and non-interest earning members of the economy an important part of her story [see also Kregel (1983a)]. All this could imply that the AD curve may not be downward sloping. Also, when W falls, there would also be shifts in income distribution between workers and other groups which could reduce aggregate demand if workers had a higher propensity to consume, thereby shifting to the left the AD curve.[62]

Fifth, Keynes argued that a fall in P could set off changes in expectations of inflation (as also possibility changes in expectations regarding wage changes). Thus a fall in P could lead to a postponement in purchases of goods with the expectation of further falls (and similarly for investment and wages). Of course, if expectations were 'normal', the opposite would be true; the point is that no general claim can be made that a fall in P would result in a greater aggregate demand due to changes in inflationary expectations. The AD curve could thus be upward rising.

Sixth, if W and P fall, and this results in a downward revision of the expected long-run rate of interest, there may be no excess supply of money which would reduce the interest rate since the demand for money may increase. The demand for money depends not just on the rate of interest, but also on the expected long-run rate of interest (since this would affect expected changes in interest rates, and hence capital gains on non-money assets). If the long-term interest rate fell, asset holders would not expect interest rates to rise and thus cause capital gains; they could thus hold the additional real quantity of money without requiring a fall in the interest rate. The Keynes effect is thus short-circuited. The floor to the interest rate could also be set by the convenience yield on money balances, as discussed above, and this could also prevent the interest rate from falling to circumvent the Keynes effect.

If, due to the existence of unemployment, W falls, the mere recognition that money wages are flexible and can vary from day to day with changes in the economy and therefore affect the future production costs of every producer will increase the general level of uncertainty in the economy. This could happen since the money wage was the main element of cost to producers, as argued by Lerner (1952), Davidson (1972), and Wells (1978, 1979b), and further and in consequence the volatility of the wage would result in a volatility of prices. This greater uncertainty, other things constant, would reduce the level of real investment in the economy, shifting the AD curve to the left. Greater uncertainty would also presumably increase the demand for liquidity in the economy, which could further reduce spending.

It thus follows that the AD curve could be upward rising, as shown in Figure 5.2. With unemployment for a given W at the intersection of the AD and AS curves, if W fell, even for a given AD, output (and hence employment) would fall.[63] But the AD could also shift to the left, further reducing output and employment. In this situation wage flexibility would increase the problem of unemployment rather than removing it. The level of P and W would fall rapidly.[64]

Under these circumstances it would be socially desirable to stabilize the money wage; the government might then respond by instituting measures, such as minimum wage legislation, which would make W rigid.[65] Individual firms and households would also enter into long-term contracts to make prices and wages more rigid, thereby reducing uncertainty. Thus the AS curve would be frozen due to wage rigidity. But the argument of the bastard Keynesians is now on its head: instead of wage rigidity causing unemployment, unemployment (and the

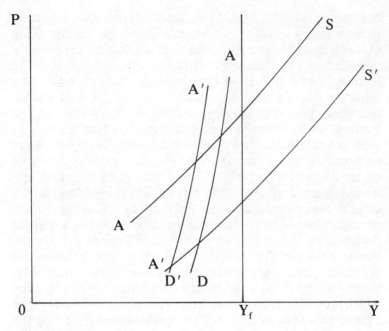

Figure 5.2

factors that cause it) cause wage rigidity! Greater wage flexibility would increase unemployment rather than reducing it; this
would be true if wage rigidity were the result of trade union
pressures or any of the other explanations that have recently
been produced to explain the observed rigidity of wages.[66]

Four comments on this analysis may be made. First, what
has been said using the aggregate demand and supply curves
here could have been said using the Z and A curves of the
standard Post Keynesian model. Wage reductions would push
the A curve down more than the Z curve, thereby increasing
unemployment if the Post Keynesian arguments were true.
However, there would be no reason to suppose that the
textbook apparatus was fundamentally flawed and, as we
have seen, could be suitably modified to represent Post
Keynesian results. In particular, since the IS–LM diagram was
used in deriving the AD curve (with some modifications), that
diagram is not necessarily inconsistent with Post Keynesian

arguments. Second, this type of formalization does suggest that the three basic features – historical time, uncertainty and money – play fundamental roles in causing unemployment equilibrium by making the AD curve upward rising and shifting. Uncertainty enters into the first, fifth, sixth and final arguments; monetary factors into the second, third, fourth and final ones; and the role of historical time everywhere. Further, with unemployment equilibrium the stage is set for uncertainty to play a role in shifting the AD curve in response to changes in the economic environment by affecting the state of long-run expectations, thereby creating instability. But wage rigidity and long-term contracts in money terms also serve to prevent excessive instability and cause the breakdown of capitalism. Third, the issues discussed here cannot be described as 'imperfections' in the sense that they are temporary or removable distortions in the workings of capitalist economies. The factors that prevent the economy from being led to full employment due to wage flexibility seem to be those which are intrinsic to the capitalist system. In particular, they cannot be simply said to require 'special cases' involving the liquidity trap or the absence of the real balance effect. Finally, we have used several different arguments to show why wage flexibility need not produce full employment. None of the arguments, in their strong form (for example a horizontal supply curve of money), are required for this result; but in combination, they do appear to provide a strong case.

CONCLUDING REMARKS

Our analysis suggests that although the work of the Post Keynesians has often been vague and repetitive (repeating Keynes and each other) and although there have sometimes been excessively strong claims made by them which cannot be sustained, the Post Keynesians have pointed to many important features of the economy which may explain why unemployment can exist in the economy for prolonged periods.

These arguments sometimes involve issues which are difficult to formalize, as testified by the slow development of models incorporating them by mainstream macroeconomists, but many of them can be incorporated into standard models to show why unemployment equilibrium can exist without wage rigidity. Not only can such exercises clarify the arguments and weed out inconsistencies and excessive claims, they can help in convincing some mainstream economists of the relevance of Post Keynesian economics. Moreover, by creating simple, teachable models, Post Keynesian economics can be popularized among students.

Even without formalizations, there remains considerable scope for extending and consolidating the Post Keynesian analysis of uncertainty, money and the treatment of time. If the recent flurry of interest in these issues is any indication, the Post Keynesian approach is healthy and developing.

NOTES

1. The name 'American post Keynesians' is inadequate since all those who are part of the group are not Americans. Coddington (1983) has used the term 'fundamentalists' to underline the fact that members of the group try to interpret Keynes's word to the letter, although he agrees with Patinkin that they do so in a selective manner to serve as a vehicle for expounding their own views. Given the somewhat pejorative sense in which this term is used, we have chosen not to use it, and instead used the term 'Post Keynesian' following the name of the major journal associated with this school, the *Journal of Post Keynesian Economics*. This nomenclature is also not without its problems, since our neo-Ricardians have also been included under the label. There are some other economists who have sometimes been called 'Post-Keynesians'. Tarshis (1980), Harcourt (1985), Carvalho (1984-5), and Hamouda and Harcourt (1988) have used the name in an even broader sense.
2. JMK, VIII. For a discussion of Keynes's notions regarding uncertainty and probability, and their relationship to the *General Theory*, see Cochrane (1971), E. Weintraub (1975) and Stohs (1980). Recently this literature has expanded rapidly: see Carabelli (1985, 1988), Lawson (1985, 1987, 1988), O'Donnell (1982), Hamouda and Smithin (1988a, b) Carvalho (1988) and Rotheim (1988). See also note 3 below.
3. Another piece of evidence comes from Bertil Ohlin, who in 1977 wrote:

In the *General Theory* . . . [Keynes] . . . emphasizes *the uncertainty of the future* and the importance of opinions about the future as a basis for action by businessmen and consumers. When he came to Stockholm in the autumn of 1936 and gave a lecture to our little Political Economy Club he – to our surprise – emphasized the analysis of this aspect of the *General Theory*. His opinion was that its vital importance had been underestimated. (Patinkin and Leith, 1977, emphasis in original)

4. Uncertainty is not completely ignored in this chapter either. In it, Keynes attacks Fisher's view of the real interest rate as given by the difference between the nominal rate of interest and the rate of inflation, where it is not clear whether the rate of inflation is foreseen or not. If it is unforeseen there will be no effect on current affairs, while if it is foreseen, the price of existing goods will already have been adjusted. If by foreseen, we mean that the future is actuarily certain, it is clear that Keynes is not ignoring uncertainty. We are grateful to Paul Davidson for pointing this out to us. See also Kahn (1984) and Carabelli (1988).

5. Sometimes Marxists of various shades are included. Hamouda and Harcourt include the contributions of Dobb, Levine and Rowthorn, among others. The strong influence of Kalecki sometimes makes it difficult to draw the line between Post Keynesians and Marxists, but we would feel extremely uneasy to include those in whose work effective demand does not play a central role among Post Keynesians.

6. Goodwin's (1967, 1982) work [see also Goodwin and Punzo (1987)] was often more Marxian than Keynesian since it tended to abstract from the problem of effective demand, but his theories can and have been extended to introduce Keynesian issues. See, for example, Skott (1989).

7. For a discussion of these contributions see Harris (1978), Marglin (1984) and Dutt (1989).

8. See Robinson (1974), (1977). For a summary of her views, see Gram and Walsh (1983). See also Asimakopulos (1978).

9. Dow (1985) also compares these three notions to Shackle's (1968) notion of expectational time which refers to the subjective perceptions of time by individuals, not to the actual flow of time.

10. Perhaps because the possibility of reversal arises in a time horizon beyond what is being considered in the analysis.

11. Recent models of hysteresis in macroeconomics also show the path-dependence of equilibrium. Blanchard and Summers (1987), for example, predict hysteresis in the unemployment rate using an insider-outsider model of union behaviour.

12. See Carabelli (1985, 1988), Carvalho (1988), Hamouda and Smithin (1988a, 1988b), Lawson (1985, 1987, 1988), O'Donnell (1982), Rotheim (1988) and Winslow (1986), for example.

13. Many Post Keynesians have stressed this distinction between atomic

and organic systems. See, for example, Brown-Collier (1985), Cara-belli (1985, 1988), Hamouda and Smithin (1988a), Rotheim (1988) and Winslow (1986).

14. The distinction between greater probability and greater confidence can be grasped as follows. The appearance – in the mind of a person – of more evidence about how unlikely a particular outcome is, may increase the degree of confidence in her or his subjective probability distribution but may not alter the probability distribution itself.

15. We shall return to these arguments below.

16. An example would be a few large losses affecting a few people (too small to affect average profitability) which would shake the confidence of businessmen they are regularly in contact with, reduce their levels of investment and thereby have a greater effect on aggregate demand, at which point firms more generally could have a loss of confidence and a change in behaviour.

17. See Dow and Dow (1985) and Lawson (1985) for a more complete discussion of Keynes's views on uncertainty and a critique of Codd-ington's position. In particular they argue that the Keynes's procedure does not imply irrational behaviour on the part of investors, if rational behaviour implies that given the knowledge that is available, there are good reasons underlying the adopted behaviour. Thus the subjectivist wedge discussed by Coddington does not imply that any type of irrational behaviour is allowed for.

18. See Kregel (1988).

19. See Lavoie (1984), Moore (1979, 1984, 1986, 1988b), Rousseas (1986), and Wray (1988). The role of banks was also emphasized by Kalecki (1971).

20. See Weintraub (1978), Kaldor and Trevithick (1981), Kaldor (1982), Moore (1979, 1984, 1988a, 1988b), Minsky (1982). The discussions are obviously related to the earlier discussions in England between the so-called Banking and Currency Schools, and the Radcliffe Committee Report. See Daugherty (1942, 1943) and Kaldor (1982).

21. See Lavoie (1984), Moore (1984) and Wray (1988) for reviews.

22. See Rousseas (1986), for example.

23. See 'Alternative Theories of the Interest Rate', *Economic Journal*, June 1937, reprinted in JMK, XIV.

24. 'The "Ex-Ante" Theory of the Rate of Interest', *Economic Journal*, December 1937, reprinted in JMK, XIV. See also Kahn's (1984, pp. 162-4) discussion. See also Foster (1986) and Moore (1988b).

25. See, however, Harcourt (1983) for a critique of the emphasis on this discussion.

26. Darity and Horn's main purpose is not to argue in favour of this notion of equilibrium but to show that wage rigidity need have nothing to do with unemployment; in this case even with involuntary unemploy-ment, since the labour market clears, there is no reason for the wage to adjust.

27. See, for example, Kaldor (1972, 1985), Robinson (1974), Shackle (1967), and Davidson (1972). The criticisms generally concern the assumptions of atomistic agents, absence of economies of scale, perfect information, etc.

28. The inapplicability of the equilibrium method is stressed more by Shackle and Minsky than by Davidson, Kregel and Weintraub, for example, who have used aggregate demand and aggregate supply curves (see below) in showing short-run equilibrium. Davidson writes in a personal communication that 'we have always argued that what is involved is shifting equilibrium and not disequilibrium . . . We believe that equilibrium exists at any moment of time but there is no persistence of a unique and stable equilibrium over time'.

29. See Shapiro (1978) for a contrary view, arguing that a neo-classical view of the economy in inherent in any equilibrium analysis, which we cannot accept.

30. Any theorizing – formal or otherwise – must involve some type of dichotomy, which implies that the theory explains the behaviour of some things (variables) and takes as given some other things (parameters) that are not explained within the theory. While stability in time (relative to the things that are being explained) could be one reason for using a dichotomy which makes certain things parameters, it is not the only one. Another one would be to make parameters things which are extremely volatile, and/or the relationship between them and the other variables is not (or cannot be) well understood. See Dutt (1986). This latter point implies that 'order' may be a stronger requirement than 'determinacy', contrary to what Carvalho (1984–5) argues.

31. In the longer run, capital accumulation, changes in preferences and wage changes may provide important examples of path-dependent equilibria.

32. It is possible to model this type of dependence. Note also that this modelling would involve the equilibrium method, as does Kregel's taxonomy. This is one example of a formal contribution that Post Keynesians can make which should attract the attention of mainstream economists, who have only recently begun grappling with problems of this type. See Hahn (1987).

33. Even models of chaos involve examining the chaotic behaviour of some short-run equilibria over time.

34. See Dow (1980).

35. It is of interest to note that Solow (1985) more recently seems to be stressing the importance of doing economics in an historical setting, a view which would put him closer to the Post Keynesian position. But here too he underscores the importance of formal model building.

36. The chapters are 3, 4, 6, 8, 10, 13, 15, 19 (appendix), 20 and 21.

37. Early presentations are reviewed by de Jong (1954a), which led to considerable discussion. See Hawtrey (1954, 1956), de Jong (1954b, 1955, 1956) and Robertson (1955, 1956). Subsequent, usually more

lucid (although not all error-free) presentations are available in Weintraub (1958), Wells (1960, 1962), Davidson and Smolensky (1964), Millar (1972), Chick (1983), and Casarosa (1981).

38. This follows Dutt (1985, 1987). See also Amadeo (1989).

39. Only in one paragraph in chapter 19 (and perhaps a hint in chapter 8) does Keynes distinguish between income classes; many post Keynesians, however, distinguish between classes in their models.

40. The interpretation is standard, essentially the same as in Weintraub (1958), Wells (1960, 1962) Marty (1961), Davidson and Smolensky (1964), Tarshis (1979) and E. R. Weintraub (1979). Patinkin's (1976) different interpretation is correctly criticized by Roberts (1978), although the former is certainly right in arguing that Keynes did not clearly state what the aggregate supply curve really was.

41. Although we use the same notation for the expected price as in chapter 2, it should be clear that the symbols have different meanings in the two chapters. In the former they referred to the expected price level for workers while here they refer to the expected price level for firms.

42. Similar interpretations are also available in Johnson's appendix to Robertson (1955) and Casarosa (1981). Johnson differs from us in not considering income distribution. Weintraub and Davidson and Smolensky consider several income groups: rentiers, wage earners and profit earners. But for these differences in model specification, they all use the price implicit in the aggregate supply function for each level of employment at which to value demand.

43. In our model if investment is fixed in nominal terms and not real terms the D(N) function would simply be given by
$$D(N) = WN + I_n$$
where I_n is the fixed level of *nominal* investment; in this case there would be no reason to worry about the price in finding the D(N) curve. But in general this is not the case.

44. Millar (1972) makes the same assumption, although he does not assume perfect competition.

45. Leijonhufvud (1974) has recanted since.

46. It should be pointed out that Hicks's (1937) paper, commonly thought to be the source of the IS–LM model, is not guilty of this error. Hicks assumes a given money wage but not a given price level.

47. See also Ambrosi (1981) and Dutt (1987). The adjustment process in the model would then go as follows: if excess demand exists in the model at any level of output, the price level rises; This causes the expected price to increase and this makes firms increase output.

48. See Kregel (1988) for a recent critique along roughly similar lines, although providing a justification of why the LM curve could not be used since it assumes that the demand for money is a stable function of the interest rate (and real income).

49. The model has also come under attack from Leijonhufvud (1968, 1981) both for diverting attention from what he considered to be the

essence of the Keynesian revolution, that is, information failure, and for introducing the stock equilibrium concept in the asset market rather than a flow one (the latter being a criticism actually of Keynes himself). See Solow (1984) for a critique of these points.

50. Thus Tobin described it as 'the trained intuition of many of us'. Solow (1984) writes that '[t]o a large extent the IS–LM model has for almost fifty years *been* Keynesian economics, though only a part of Keynesian economics it is fair to say'.

51. This is not to imply that Post Keynesians do not always follow up their discussion of the model with arguments showing why reductions in money wages may not increase employment.

52. Yellen (1980) has used the reasoning to criticize a slightly different Post Keynesian model. But as the next section shows, her final judgement on the absence of any role of money in the Post Keynesian model is completely misplaced.

53. One can argue that it has some disadvantages. By not measuring the price on some axis the Post Keynesian diagram does not show explicitly its level; this may have been at the root of some of the problems and inconsistencies regarding the market price and the expected price, as discussed above, which have plagued many discussions of this diagram. There is no evidence that these problems are disappearing. See for example, Torr (1984) and Casarosa (1984).

54. The following follows Dutt (1985).

55. Patinkin (1982) has argued that Keynes did not use unit price and physical quantities because these indexes were not widely used in his time.

56. This follows Dutt (1986–7). The issues discussed are not new; many of them are to be found in Keynes (JMK, VII), and in the work of many Post Keynesians, including Davidson and Smolensky (1965).

57. This argument, denying that investment responds inversely to the interest rate, is the common point between the Post Keynesians and neo-Ricardian Keynesians. However, while Post Keynesians would argue in terms of uncertainty and long-term expectations, the latter would argue it on the basis of the heterogeneity of capital goods, as shown above.

58. See Carabelli (1988, pp. 200–1).

59. See also Howitt (1986) for a formal model.

60. See Presley (1986). Keynes seems to have had an important role in Robertson's development of the argument.

61. Note that if this is thought to be due to the interest elasticity of investment and the real balance effect, and our analysis in the two previous paragraphs is correct, it may be thought that no reductions in aggregate demand would occur. However, Post Keynesians could try to have it both ways, and with reason, thanks to possible ratchet effects. It could be argued that an increase in the rate of interest could reduce investment and not the other way around; similarly for a fall in real balances.

62. This comes out more clearly in a Kaleckian model. See Dutt (1984, 1989) for an analysis.
63. Keynes assumed that the real wage was equal to the marginal product of labour in equilibrium. This implies that if output and employment fall due to the fall in the money wage, the price level would have to fall more, thereby increasing the real wage. McCombie (1985-6) has pointed out, however, that the real wage does not have to increase if the money wage reduction results in a fall in employment. This is because if a reduction in aggregate demand results in a lower utilization of capacity, the marginal production of labour curve can shift downwards so that a lower real wage can be compatible with a lower level of employment. Short-run analysis precludes increases in the stock of capital but is not incompatible with a lower utilization of capital services.
64. This is strongly reminiscent of Keynes's own discussion of the subject. For example, '. . . very small fluctuations in the propensity to consume and the inducement to invest would cause money-prices to rush violently between zero and infinity' (p. 239), and '. . . prices would be in an unstable equilibrium . . . racing to zero whenever investment was below [the critical level], and to infinity whenever it was above it . . .' (pp. 269-70).
65. As Keynes (JMK, VII, p. 269) notes:

    The chief result of . . . [a flexible wage] policy would be to cause a great instability of prices, so violent perhaps as to make business calculations futile in an economic society functioning after the manner of that in which we live. To suppose that a flexible wage policy is a right and proper adjunct of a system which on the whole is one of *laissez-faire*, is the opposite of the truth.

66. See, for example, Solow (1979).

6. The Neo-Ricardian Keynesians and the Post Keynesians Compared

INTRODUCTION

Having examined the analysis of the neo-Ricardian Keynesians and the Post Keynesians in turn, we are now in a position to examine them in a comparative manner.

DIFFERENCES

Since the economists belonging to each group have tried to distinguish sharply their product from those of the other, and in fact have shown open hostility to the work of the other group,[1] it seems more natural to start by comparing the main differences in the approach and analysis of the two groups.

Any such comparison would seem to have to take into account the possible dangers of such a venture due to the fact that the two groups supposedly work within two alternative research programmes. This fact could possibly imply that they pose different questions and speak different languages, making any comparison tricky business. The neo-Ricardian Keynesians clearly belong to a research programme which takes the Sraffian prices of production approach, with its implied dichotomy and the equalization of rates of profit concept of equilibrium, as its hard core. The Post Keynesians have also argued that they have their own 'paradigm' [see Eichner and Kregel (1975)],[2] and at least one non-Post Keynesian has been willing to recognize the existence of a Post

147

Keynesian research programme.[3] While it is possible to list some issues which the group consider important, the hard core of this research programme seems not to have been defined, and we do not believe can be defined in terms as easily as other programmes which have a unified formal theoretical structure, since the Post Keynesians are interested more in the implications of certain concepts rather than in tools of analysis.[4] Consequently, we feel entitled to overlook this problem. Further, in what we are concerned with, both groups seem to be dealing with at least one indentical question – the existence of unemployment – and there is no reason to believe that they define unemployment in different ways.

For purposes of comparison, it is convenient to return to the four issues that have been discussed by the Post Keynesians: time, uncertainty, money and equilibrium, and then to compare their explanations of the existence of unemployment.

Regarding time, the neo-Ricardian Keynesians regard it as logical time, and the Post Keynesians insist on historical time. We have already argued that one's attitude to the treatment of time ultimately reduces to one's attitude towards uncertainty and the nature of equilibrium, and so there is no reason to believe that apart from differences arising from these issues there can be any difference regarding the attitudes to time.

Regarding uncertainty and the formation of expectations, the Post Keynesians have given it a central role in their analysis. Regarding the neo-Ricardian Keynesians, they do not deny the existence of uncertainty and the necessity of taking into consideration the fact that individuals can form expectations about the future.[5] What they deny is that expectational issues – which are subjective – have any bearing on long-period equilibrium in their sense – which is determined by objective factors. The former could have a bearing on the study of questions relating to the deviation from long-period equilibrium, but nothing definite could be said about the behaviour of the economy during such deviations because nothing definite could be said about expectations. Since economists need definite results, they should ignore any position out of long-period equilibrium and thus should not overemphasize the role of uncertainty and expectations.

There seem to be two separate issues that divide the two groups. First, there is the issue as to whether 'short-period' phenomena which admittedly depend on expectations can be studied in a systematic manner. While the neo-Ricardian Keynesians deny this, their denial is made on the basis of how they define 'systematic', which is defined internally in their research programme as positions of long-period equilibrium in their sense; also, their analysis is not contradictory with an analysis of such transient phenomena, only that they choose not to make it. The Post Keynesians, in not following the same definition of systematic, and sometimes going to the extent of saying that economies are inherently unstable and thus should not be described by systematic relations, have taken the step of analysing short-period phenomena and hence expectational issues in their analysis.

Second, there is the issue as to whether expectational issues and uncertainty have a bearing on the long-period equilibrium position of the neo-Ricardians, and that by ignoring history (that is, the actual path of the economy) they have a mistaken notion of long-period equilibrium.[6] Logically the neo-Ricardian Keynesians cannot be faulted on this ground since by taking, for instance, output levels as given, they may already have taken into account the role of history in the given levels of output, without denying the effect of history in determining them (in an unspecified and unknown manner). We therefore conclude that there is no necessary contradiction between the two groups in their attitudes towards uncertainty and expectations. One group has merely chosen not to analyse short-period phenomena because of its transitory nature, while the other group has decided to take such a step. Whether such a step is forward or backward seems to have no real bearing on the criticisms that each group makes of the other.

Regarding money, the Post Keynesians give it centre stage in their analysis, while it finds no place in the neo-Ricardian Keynesian core. Nevertheless, the neo-Ricardian Keynesians have realized the need to incorporate money into their analysis to explain certain crucial features of the real world. We have already referred to Sraffa's (1960) comment that monetary factors would determine the distribution of income, through the interest rate, and as we have seen in chapter 4, some economists working in the neo-Ricardian tradition have pursued the matter further.[7] However, the neo-Ricardian Keynesians have not analysed the implications of having money for the analysis of output and employment since they have not examined in a systematic manner the relationship between distribution and output, both considered to be given in their analysis. This does not consist of a denial of the role of money in questions relating to unemployment but at most a claim that nothing 'systematic' can be said about such a relationship.

Regarding equilibrium, the Post Keynesians and neo-Ricardian Keynesians seem to have gone to two extremes. The former have insisted that economics can only be studied in terms of long-period equilibrium positions, while the latter have analysed short-period behaviour of capitalist economies, and in studying their inherent instability have sometimes denied the applicability of the equilibrium method to economics. The neo-Ricardian Keynesians are probably right to the extent of arguing that if an equilibrium concept is not employed, nothing definite can be said regarding the economy; we have argued that some of the Post Keynesians, by denying the notion of equilibrium, seem to have gone too close to nihilism, and that their arguments can be couched in terms of equilibrium analysis, as shown in the previous chapter. But the neo-Ricardian Keynesians have gone too far to deny any notion of equilibrium other than their own, which fixes the level and composition of output, distribution (wage or profit) and technology, and finds prices which equalize rates of profit. Even if their equilibrium is a useful one to consider, there is no logical reason why some other equilibrium position cannot be studied which has a different set of exogenous variables.[8] A Post Keynesian notion of equilibrium could thus be thought to be consistent with a larger set of data (since in a shorter-time horizon more things could be said to be given, following Marshall, as discussed in chapter 3 above). And it is possible that in some cases, the neo-Ricardian dichotomy (with a particular specification of the data set) is not a useful one.[9] This may occur if we believe that there is no long run which is truly independent of the short run, so that the long-run equilibrium is either some average of so-called short-run equilibria or dependent on the path traced by the short-run equilibria over time.[10] In this case we could still analyse the long-period equilibria in the neo-Ricardian manner but the usefulness of the exercise would be limited since we would not be able to explain why the output levels were what they were. We will return to this issue later in this chapter. We conclude that regarding their attitudes towards equilibrium, there is a difference separating the two groups, but due to reasons that cannot be sustained. The Post Keynesians need not jettison the notion of equilibrium, and the neo-Ricardian Keynesians can use their particular characterization of equilibrium without denying the existence of others.

Finally, there are differences in the arguments that the neo-Ricardian Keynesians and Post Keynesians provide on the reasons for the existence of unemployment and the flaws in the neo-classical claim of an automatic tendency toward full employment. The neo-Ricardian Keynesians seem to rely exclusively on the notion of capital heterogeneity which could make investment not be a downward-sloping function of the interest rate. Thus, with unemployment, if the money wage fell, and so did the interest rate, the level of investment demand need not rise to take the economy to full employment. Notice that this only denies the necessary operation of the 'Keynes effect'. The Post Keynesians have provided a richer menu of arguments, relating to uncertainty and expectations, to income distributional shifts, to the role of monetary institutions, to negate the neo-classical argument. Their arguments not only show that investment need not be an inverse function of the interest rate (using expectational arguments) but also that falling money wages may prevent a fall in interest rates (both arguments negating the Keynes effect), and that falling wages and prices could reduce aggregate demand in other ways, offsetting even any possible 'real balance effect'. However, the point to note here is that there is no inconsistency between the neo-Ricardian Keynesian and the Post Keynesian arguments and neither group relies on wage rigidity to explain unemployment.

SIMILARITIES

From the foregoing we are led to believe that there seem to be no sustainable contradictions between the neo-Ricardian Keynesians and the Post Keynesians,[11] only a difference as to the reasons why the economy will not be led to full employment by market forces.[12] In fact, as we now argue, there are some fundamental similarities between the two groups.

The first is the fundamental similarity that neither of the two groups is saying that the economy does not achieve full employment due to some imperfections in the workings of the market. Some varieties of Keynesianism do argue that unemployment exists due to wage (and/or price) rigidity, and have led economists and policy makers to believe that the removal of such imperfections would solve the problem of unemployment. The neo-Ricardian Keynesian argument follows from the fact of capital goods heterogeneity: this is a fact that cannot be removed, except by a government that invents one machine that can do everything and abolishes all other kinds of machinery! The Post Keynesian argument shows how wage–price changes will do nothing to cure unemployment. Uncertainty, banks, and the existence of different groups (workers, rentiers, capitalists, firms) with different behaviour patterns are not market imperfections which can be removed. Thus the removal of restrictions on wages and prices (by breaking unions or by promoting competition in goods markets) would not deliver the economy from unemployment.

We here object vehemently to the assertion made by some neo-Ricardian Keynesians [Eatwell and Milgate (1983), Magnani (1983)] that the Post Keynesians are 'imperfectionists'.[13] If by 'perfect' one defines the world portrayed by the neo-classical general equilibrium system which leads to full employment equilibrium, then by definition anyone who argues that the economy can experience unemployment for a 'long' period of time (both types of Keynesians we are considering fit the bill) is an 'imperfectionist'. Alternatively, if by 'perfect' one defines the textbook neo-classical synthesis model with all its functions having regularly signed partial derivatives with respect to their arguments, and with all prices perfectly flexible, both types of Keynesians turn out to be imperfectionists, the neo-Ricardian Keynesians by arguing that the investment schedule is not downward sloping, and the Post Keynesians with the same argument and by showing that the interest rate need not fall (due to the 'perversities' in the demand for money function or the endogeneity of money supply). By calling the Post Keynesians imperfectionists, the neo-Ricardian Keynesians become imperfectionists, too. Actually, both the definitions of imperfectionist (which roughly amount to the same) imply a neo-classical view of perfectionism, which is a theoretical one, based, as it is, on concepts which are sensible only within a neo-classical research programme. More generally, if we define imperfections as those factors which interfere with the free forces of the market that can, in principle, be removed without destroying the free markets (by breaking unions and monopolies)[14] neither of the two groups are imperfectionists.[15] The neo-Ricardians may still insist that they have destroyed the neo-classical argument by showing the neo-classical system to be inconsistent. This is a claim that we cannot entertain.[16]

Second, both groups could be interpreted as not only saying that unemployment is not the result of rigidities but that removal of rigidities (which exist for whatever reasons) could destabilize the economy and increase unemployment. The Post Keynesians argue this point explicitly, as shown in chapter 5. If money wages become perfectly flexible, the economy would be subjected to wide fluctuations and uncertainty would increase, confounding the problem of unemployment. The neo-Ricardian Keynesians do not make the point explicit, but the argument can be distilled from their work. Suppose that the capital employment schedule is upward rising and less steep than the saving schedule (as drawn in Figure 4.5a). Then if there is an excess of saving over investment, the interest rate would fall, increasing the gap. The interest rate would just not be an adjusting variable, and the level of output and employment would have to fall. But if interest rates change quickly and output takes more time to adjust, the economy would become highly unstable with the interest rate falling without limit. This would not destroy the neo-Ricardian Keynesian result that unemployment would exist but make the economy seem more unstable than it actually is. Sraffa's solution was to suggest that the interest rate was made rigid by the monetary authorities. But this is not the *cause* of unemployment. Removal of the rigidity of the interest rate would *increase* uncertainty in the economy, and presumably, unemployment!

REASONS FOR DISAGREEMENT

Our conclusion from this comparison of the analysis of the two types of Keynesians suggests that there is no necessary contradiction between the two groups. The question still remains as to why they have quarrelled so much.[17] The reason, we believe, can be attributed to two factors.

The first has to do with the sociology of science. It may be argued that there exists a natural tendency in minorities to look for their roots and find ways to establish their identities. Economists are no exception. Marx tried to differentiate his product by calling almost anything written before he started writing 'bourgeoise Political Economy'. Keynes similarly gave the name 'classical' to a group of economists ranging from Ricardo to Pigou. Radical economists in both the Marxian and Keynesian traditions also try to emphasize the differences between their ideas and those of mainstream economists. In doing this there is a strong tendency to go back to the original text (Marx's *Capital* or Keynes's *General Theory*), and to identify (in their opinion) *truly* Marxian and Keynesian conceptions.

The two varieties of Keynesians we are considering in this book explore different dimensions of Keynes's *General Theory*. In a word, the Post Keynesians emphasize the role of money and uncertainty whereas the neo-Ricardian Keynesians emphasize the multiplier mechanism and the role of output as the equilibrating variable between saving and investment, since such equilibrating is not provided by the interest rate due to the heterogeneity of capital goods. By doing this they are, in fact, searching for their identities. They are focusing their analyses on what they consider to be the truly innovative or revolutionary elements of Keynes's ideas. One important reason for the existence of two groups of non-mainstream Keynesians is the fact that Keynes himself emphasized the notions of unemployment equilibrium (for which the role of the multiplier is central) and the instability of the system (for which the role of money and uncertainty are fundamental).

The second has to do with ideology. Some of the Post Keynesians have expressed a belief in the workings of the private enterprise system if it could be controlled in specified ways, that is, by control of the banking and financial systems, and with incomes and price policies.[18] Some of these prescriptions have to do with their analysis of the ills of the private enterprise system, as discussed above. Some of the neo-Ricardian Keynesians, on the other hand, have expressed a more fundamental distrust in the workings of the free market and this is obviously related to their belief that they have shown the inconsistency of the neo-classical adjustment mechanism. What belief one has in the efficacy of the free market system is based on one's ideology. While ideology could drive one to this camp or that, it should be realized that it does not logically imply the acceptance of a particular type of economic analysis. The neo-Ricardian Keynesians have not shown that the free market system does not work (or cannot be made to work); at best, they have shown that the neo-classical demonstration is flawed. The Post Keynesians have not shown that the free market system could be suitably modified to make it work; they might suffer from naïveté about political realities and class conflicts, and a consequently mistaken (or overly optimistic) view of the state and its ability or willingness to resolve the problem of unemployment.[19]

TOWARDS A RECONCILIATION

We therefore argue that there is no necessary contradiction between the two groups. The implication of this is that there should be some sort of reconciliation between them. However, this reconciliation must take into account the differences between them.

It follows from our analysis that the type of reconciliation we have in mind is for the two groups to concentrate their research on the issues that interest them the most, the neo-Ricardians on the implications of the heterogeneity of capital goods in the long period, and the Post Keynesians on uncertainty, money and historical time. In these endeavours their primary task can be seen as building theoretical approaches alternative to the neo-classical approach, which undermine the conclusions of the latter. If these approaches can show that free markets do not automatically result in full employment or that it is not possible to achieve full employment by removing wage rigidities through weaking labour, they will have achieved a great deal. There are different possible routes to follow in demonstrating this, and there is no need to believe that there is one exclusive way. To emphasize one way is to bring it into sharper focus theoretical purposes, not necessarily to imply that some other way is unimportant.

A further issue is that the two types of approaches, as they develop to analyse additional kinds of issues, may each find it useful to borrow concepts and ideas from the other approach. Consider some examples. First, as we have seen in chapter 4, neo-Ricardians have tried explicitly to introduce monetary factors in trying to analyse the determination of the interest rate. Here they can use some of the analysis developed by the Post Keynesians. They may also wish to analyse the implications of movements of the economy out of their long period, and to see whether the long period centres of gravitation are stable or not. Here too they may use some of the Post Keynesian ideas on the adjustment of expectations and quantities. Post Keynesians have also analysed the implications of their analysis for accumulation over longer periods. But much of this analysis remains in a macroeconomic setting, assuming one commodity. A useful extension would be to allow for many sectors and for the heterogeneity of capital goods. Here the neo-Ricardian idea of the uniform rate of profit and the prices of production may come in useful. It should be stressed that these are meant to be illustrative examples of types of analysis which are possible, not as recommendations of a synthesis in all theorizing. As we have argued, by focusing on some sets of issues and ignoring others these schools have brought these issues into sharper focus.

Other than making comments we would not wish to push the idea of a synthesis too far. It is likely that a forced attempt at such a reconciliation which does not take into account the methodological differences between the two groups is bound to end in failure. To illustrate this we conclude with a discussion of two recent recommendations for synthesis that have been made which, in our opinion, are not warranted. These have been made by Dow (1985) and by McKenna and Zannoni (1987).

Dow's (1985, pp. 101–5) recommendation can be interpreted as suggesting that Post Keynesians consider the short period and the neo-Ricardian Keynesians emphasize the long period, and that macroeconomic analysis can borrow mainly from the former in analysing the short period and from the latter in analysing the long period. This overlooks the important fact that Post Keynesian analysis in the long period may turn out to be very different from the type of the long-period analysis conducted by the neo-Ricardians. We have already noted that Post Keynesians often take the view that the 'long period' is not independent of the short period. This can either be taken to mean the path-dependence of long-period equilibrium, or it can be taken to imply that the long period is nothing but some sort of average of the short periods.[20] It follows then that the long-period equilibrium in the Post Keynesian sense may actually be affected by short-period developments or share the properties of short-period equilibrium, both claims being inconsistent with neo-Ricardian analysis which analyses long-period position *independently* of the short-period behaviour of the economy. The implications of this for a specific model have been explored in Dutt (1986, 1989), where a two-sector model is considered with a long-period steady state, equalized rate of profit equilibrium. However, a typically short-period feature, the existence of excess capacity of fixed capital, is assumed. It is shown that although formally there is a Sraffian pricing apparatus embedded in the model, these equations do not 'determine' relative prices, since the capital–output ratios are not parameters in the model but are determined by aggregate demand in a Kalecki–Keynesian manner. Moreover, the implications of the model are anti-neo-Ricardian since it implies that a higher real wage is associated with a higher rate of profit *contra* the inverse relations between the two distributional variables in Sraffa's analysis. The analysis is much closer to, for example, Joan Robinson's (1937) analysis of the long period.

McKenna and Zannoni (1987) have argued that Post Keynesians should replace their confusing marginal physical productivity of labour (MPL) concept by the neo-Ricardian uniform rate of profit (URP) concept, thereby bringing the two approaches closer together. In addition to the fact that there is no necessary problem with the MPL notion in Post Keynesian economics,[21] and that the URP and MPL are not substitutes in the sense that one can be replaced by the other in a model, [22] this suggestion ignores the fact that there are important differences between the vision underlying the neo-Ricardian URP concept and the Post Keynesian perspective, as noted above. The URP concept involved adopting the long-period equilibrium approach which according to Eatwell and Milgate (1983) 'captures the persistent and systematic forces that work through competition' towards the equalization of profit rates. As we have seen above, this particular conception of long-period position implies the adoption of a particular position regarding the treatment of uncertainty in neo-Ricardian theory. As Eatwell and Milgate (1983) express it:

The influence of uncertainty is just one of those multitude of influences which cause the day-to-day circumstances of the economy to deviate from the long run normal operation. Uncertainty and expectations may thus be confined to the category of 'temporary' or non-systematic effects, as distinct from the persistent and systematic forces which act to determine the long-run position.

Since the Post Keynesians believe that no serious study of capitalist economies is possible by ignoring uncertainty they would be unwilling to make the URP notion an integral part of their theory. This is testified by some of the reactions by Post Keynesians to the McKenna–Zannoni paper.[23]

NOTES

1. For the neo-Ricardian Keynesians writing against the Post Keynesians, see, for example, Eatwell and Milgate (1983) Introduction, and Magnani (1983); for Post Keynesians against the Neo-Ricardian Keynesians, see Asimakopulos (1985).
2. We should hasten to add that Eichner and Kregel define the paradigm more broadly than we have, not excluding the neo-Ricardian Keynesians and including those who have extended Keynes's work.
3. See E. Weintraub (1985).
4. Part of the reason lies in the widely different backgrounds of those who have made contributions to the approach. There is no implication that there is thus a weakness in the Post Keynesian approach. In fact, it could be considered to be a strength, in not shackling them to any particular research programme and thereby reducing their creativity.
5. See Kregel (1976) for an interpretation.
6. It is easy to see that if there are irreversibilities in the movement of some variable outside equilibrium, the equilibrium position will depend on the path taken by the economy. We have discussed this case in chapter 5.
7. See Panico (1980, 1985) and Pivetti (1985) for further analysis.
8. Perhaps Eatwell and Milgate (1983) would not disagree, since they write that

[i]t is important to stress that our arguments should not be mistaken for the advocacy of . . . 'long period analysis' to the exclusion of everything else. The true point is rather different – it is that if one wishes to conduct an adequate 'disequilibrium' analysis one must first be satisfied with the equilibrium analysis from which the disequilibrium is *necessarily* derived . . . (emphasis in original).

We should add that what they call disequilibrium analysis may be an equilibrium analysis with a different set of exogenous elements, and that Post Keynesians may deny the last part of this statement and instead posit that the 'equilibrium' must be studied only as an outcome of the 'disequilibrium' path and history must play a role.
9. See Dutt (1986, 1989). See also the section below entitled 'Towards a reconciliation'.
10. See also Kregel (1983b, pp. 50–1).
11. We come to a conclusion similar to that of Dow (1985, pp. 105–6) who argues that the Post Keynesians (in our terminology) focus on the short run and the neo-Ricardian Keynesians focus on the long run, so that the two can be combined into an analysis which focuses both on the short and long runs. Our analysis, examining several different issues, obviously went into the similarities and differences between the two groups in much more detail in coming to this same conclusion.

12. We should repeat that we do not imply that there are no (in some sense) fundamental differences between the two groups. Carvalho (1984—5) stresses these differences, and argues that they are rooted in the 'vision' adopted by each group and we would agree with much of his analysis. What we do argue is that both views make positive contributions which, when appropriately interpreted, are not necessarily in contradiction with each other.

13. Milgate has pointed out in personal communication that they (Eatwell and he) have not explicitly called the Post Keynesians 'imperfectionists'. We believe that when they state that 'inefficiencies introduced into the working of the "real" economy by the working of the monetary system' provide an example of an imperfection, they are in effect doing so, although they may have had Arrow and Hahn (1971) in mind in giving this example. Magnani (1983) is more explicit.

14. The force of this argument is reduced somewhat by the fact that someone would argue that such 'rigidities' are intrinsic parts of free markets and by removing them free markets would ultimately collapse. We still believe that our definition of imperfection serves some purpose.

15. Magnani (1983) seems to misrepresent the Post Keynesians (particularly Davidson) on many particular points. For example, while the Post Keynesians do argue that uncertainty results in wage rigidity, they do not argue that wage rigidity causes unemployment. Further, the Post Keynesians are right in their critique of the fixed-price disequilibrium theories, despite Magnani's claim. While in some of their models, a fall in the real wage in response to unemployment would increase unemployment, this happens because of assumed price rigidities (sometimes just taken as given, and sometimes argued on the basis of imperfections in competition). If prices and wages were completely flexible in these models, the economies would converge to the Walrasian equilibrium. This is because they overemphasize the real balance effect and leave out of consideration all the factors considered to be important by the Post Keynesians.

16. The neo-Ricardians at best have shown that the economy may not converge to a neo-classical full-employment equilibrium. But they have also not shown that their own equilibrium with intersectorally equalized profit rates is a stable one. See, for example, Hahn (1982) and Dutt (1989).

17. Dow (1985, p. 103) states that this is caused in large part by the

insistence by some that only neo-Ricardian analysis is admissible, and others that only short-period analysis is admissible, [reflecting] the pervasiveness of the Cartesian/Euclidian mode of thought, even among those who reject it in most aspects of their work; it encourages the notion of an exclusively correct scientific procedure. (See also chapter 7, below.)

This has the problem of not explaining why this mode of thought is so pervasive. We believe it more helpful to seek for other reasons.
18. See Davidson (1972), for example.
19. The Post Keynesians are closer to Keynes in this regard. In the concluding chapter of the *General Theory*, entitled 'Concluding notes on the social philosophy towards which the General Theory might lead', Keynes states that while his theory

> indicates the vital importance of establishing certain central controls in matters which are now left in the main to individual initiative, there are wide fields of activity which are unaffected . . . [A] somewhat comprehensive socialisation of investment will prove the only means of securing an approximation to full employment . . . But beyond this no obvious case is made out for a system of State Socialism which would embrace most of the economic life of the community . . . [T]here will still remain a wide field for the exercise of private initiative and responsibility. Within this field the traditional advantages of individualism will still hold good . . . [These advantages] are partly advantages of efficiency – the advantages of decentralisation and of the play of self-interest. But above all, individualism, if it can be purged of its defects and its abuses, is the best safeguard of personal liberty in the sense that, compared with any other system, it greatly widens the field for the exercise of personal choice. (JMK, VII, pp. 377–80)

> The Post Keynesians thus take Keynes's ideological position which of course involves the making of value judgements which are not related to the rest of the *General Theory*.

20. This may be taken to be the theoretical implication of Keynes's famous dictum that 'in the long run we are all dead'. The interpretation also seems follow from Kalecki's work (see chapter 2).
21. See the discussion in chapter 4, above.
22. It is possible to construct balanced-growth multisector models which allow substitution in production in which profit rates are intersectorally equalized *and* the wage is equal to the marginal product of labour [see Hahn (1982) and Marglin (1984)]. Further, if we consider fixed coefficients models which jettison the concept of MPL altogether, the URP notion cannot by itself 'close' the model; additional behavioural assumptions are necessary, as discussed in Marglin (1984) and Dutt (1989).
23. See, for example, Brothwell (1987). Eichner (1987) and Kregel (1987).

7. Conclusion

In this book we attempted to compare the contributions of two Keynesian schools of thought whose primary objective is to provide an explanation for the phenomenon of unemployment. As noted in chapter 2, unemployment is not really an important item in the agenda of modern orthodox macroeconomics, except for the case of the more Keynesian-oriented members of the mainstream. The latter, however, have laid the blame for unemployment on money-wage rigidity. In fact in the early 1940s, the young Keynesians such as Modigliani, Patinkin and Haberler had already put forward an interpretation of Keynes's analysis which focused on wage-rigidity. In the 1970s, this view was reflected in the literature surrounding the debate over the rational expectations approach. Indeed, the Keynesian response to the rational expectations revolution was based on the notion that labour-market institutions were responsible for the rigidity of wages. By 1987, it had become clear that the main difference between the new classical and the Keynesian approach to macroeconomics was the latter's assumption of wage rigidity.

Post Keynesians have emphasized the ambiguous effects of reductions in money-wages due, for example, to its effects on the state of confidence (and, hence, on the interest rate and the inducement to invest) and on the distribution of income. In fact, on these grounds an argument can be made that the rigidity of wages may very well be a consequence rather than a cause of unemployment. The neo-Ricardians, on the other hand, have pointed out that due to the shape of the capital employment function it is not necessarily true that a reduction in money-wages (and, hence, a reduction in the interest rate) will lead to a full-employment equilibrium position.

162

Recently, prominent mainstream economists such as Tobin, Hahn and Solow, have re-examined the question of money-wage reductions and their conclusions have been quite similar to those of Keynes and the Post Keynesians. However, these analyses usually do not refer to the Post Keynesian writings reflecting, perhaps, a problem of communication between Keynesians of different varieties.

In the 1950s and 60s, the contributions of the Cambridge (UK) economists (Robinson, Kaldor, Sraffa, Kahn) were taken into account by the American Keynesians – recall the 'Cambridge controversy'. However, the second and third generations of Cambridge economists (or those economists with an intellectual attachment with Cambridge, UK) became gradually marginalized. In fact, Post Keynesianism and neo-Ricardianism are confined to small groups in the US and Italy respectively – although they are represented in small numbers elsewhere. What seems to be the problem?

Some of the reasons are associated with the fact that neo-Ricardians and Post Keynesians have difficulties in communicating between themselves. In chapter 6 we referred to aspects associated with the 'sociology of science' and 'ideology' as potential explanations for this lack of communication. The neo-Ricardian Keynesians and the Post Keynesians, while recognizing their paradigmatic differences, could devote more time and effort to understanding each other and to building some bridges between the two research agendas.

The lack of communication with mainstream economists is probably due to other causes. First, there is the 'methodological morality' of neo-classical economics [see Dow (1980)] which leads the neo-classicals to look down upon non-mathematical approaches. Students, especially in North American universities, infected by this morality and dazzled by mathematical pyrotechnics, are more interested in fashionable mathematical modelling which results in dissertations by assumption-modification rather than grappling with unfashionable and difficult issues which cannot be elegantly modelled. Dow (1985) argues that this difference between neo-classicals and our two types of Keynesians rises from a methodological difference. Mainstream neo-classicals belong to a tradition which she calls Cartesian–Euclidian, which uses an axiomatic approach and attempts to explain all economic phenomena in terms of one analytical framework. The Post Keynesians and neo-Ricardian Keynesians, however, belong to the Babylonian tradition, which realizes the futility of trying to explain all phenomena in terms of one unified framework and attempts to have partial explanations of different problems. Dow appears to take the view that Babylonianism is necessarily inconsistent with mathematical modelling but it would appear quite possible to formulate partial models to analyse particular problems with different structures and different sets of exogenous variables in each model;[1] it seems to us that there is no *necessary* link between method (methodological individualism or use of neo-classical general equilibrium models) and form (whether mathematics is used or not). Carabelli (1985, 1988) argues, however, that Keynes's views on chance, probability and uncertainty led him to a method in which economic knowledge on the part of the economist was bounded by limited knowledge and uncertainty; economic analysis did not produce necessary results, but showed that certain outcomes were possible. Just as probability could not be measured numerically, economic analysis could not be modelled mathematically; such analysis would have to use common language and its main purpose was to persuade. The problems with taking this as a justification of eschewing formalism are two-fold. First, just as in the case of individual behaviour under uncertainty individuals used the convention of using mathematical probabilities, it is possible to justify mathematical modelling as a convention, not as a depiction of reality but as an illustration of a particular view of it in a precise manner. Second, if the purpose of economic theory is to persuade, and if people get persuaded by mathematical models and not by ordinary language, there is a strong case to use the mathematical metaphor. Post Keynesians deal with problems which are difficult to model but, as argued in chapter 5, some of the problems can be modelled and an effort should be made in this direction. Some of the issues treated by the neo-Ricardians are presented in models; their writings on capital theory and international trade are the best example here. However, their apparatus is quite restricted to the Sraffian *problematique* which makes the application of the neo-Ricardian notions very narrow.

A second cause of lack of communication with main-stream economists seems, in the case of the neo-Ricardians, to stem from a cumulative process between the restrictiveness of the analytical apparatus and of the research agenda. The latter is centred in what Garegnani has referred to as the 'core' of the classical system, that is, the process of determination of the prices of production given the methods of production, one of the distribution variables and the level and composition of output. The core of the system is too narrow and therefore restricts the neo-Ricardian analysis to a very small number of economic problems. Furthermore, neo-Ricardians have been quite timid in expanding their approach to problems which are not in the core because they believe, somewhat over-cautiously perhaps, that they do not have the same degree of 'logical necessity' as those in the core. The narrowness of the agenda makes the communication between the neo-Ricardians and the mainstream economists very difficult.

Third, the Post Keynesian research agenda, on the other hand, is not well defined, and allows almost every problem to fit in it. While this has the advantage that it does not unduly restrict the set of issues and methods which are permissible, it does not provide a sufficiently clear set of 'positive heuristics'. This implies that Post Keynesians often tend to rely on the heuristic of not being neo-classical,[2] and spending too much time on vague discussions of the meaning of the fundamental tenets rather than on constructive theoretical developments.

Fourth, a significant methodological barrier separates the Post Keynesians and neo-Ricardians from mainstream economic theory. That is, their theorizing without using explicit optimization on the part of economic agents. Mainstream neo-classical economics takes as one of its basic methodological principles explanation in terms of individual optimizing behaviour. This is not so much an empirical claim of individual rationality (for rational behaviour could sometimes imply satisficing rather than optimizing, and optimizing behaviour with unreasonable constraints could result in irrational behaviour), but a methodological dictate that *all* economic behaviour *must* be explained in this way. This is not to say that mainstream economists have always followed this dictate, since they have often introduced 'distortions' and behavioural functions as 'primitives' rather than basing them on optimizing behaviour. For example, the Walrasian auctioneer, so necessary for perfectly competitive markets, does not optimize! Keynes's agents did act rationally, as discussed in chapter 5 for instance, although this need not be shown with explicit optimization. In the neo-Ricardian analysis, in which classes are emphasized rather than individuals, and class often determined behaviour, there is no necessary implication that behaviour is irrational. It is simply conditioned by the objective conditions within which individuals find themselves. Aside from the issue of optimization itself, implicit in this approach is methodological individualism – that macroeconomic behaviour must be explained in terms of individual behaviour. Post Keynesians, given their roots in Keynes's own method, would have trouble with methodological individualism. Carabelli (1988) argues that Keynes's views on uncertainty and his acceptance of the organic rather than the atomistic hypothesis (as discussed in chapter 5 above) would make it unacceptable for him to use methodological individualism. As Dow (1985) argues, his analysis, indeed, had many examples of the fallacy of composition (such as the paradox of thrift), whereby the consequences of individuals' actions in aggregate undermined individual plans, and this meant that group behaviour, rather than individual behaviour, was often the relevant starting point. Indeed, in discussion of the consumption function, investment and the demand for liquidity he refers to groups rather than individual agents, and it is only subsequent generations of Keynesians who have sought to provide the individual optimizing underpinnings. So also the neo-Ricardians, given their classical-Marxian roots, take social groups and classes as the starting point rather than individual behaviour [see Dow (1985)]; in economies where institutions and classes matter, and this may arguably be the case in most economies, it does not make good sense not to examine different behaviour between different groups. There seem to be no convincing reasons why individual optimizing behaviour is the only starting point of all economic analysis.[3] In many contexts and problems its use may be suitable and highly enlightening. But it appears that in many others, by insisting on its universal applications, it results only in carrying around excess baggage; and very often in actual use, by ruling out fallacies of composition, the proper analysis of behaviour under uncertainty and limited knowledge, and by ignoring the role of classes and institutions, it can be most inadequate.[4] We would argue, therefore, that where necessary individual optimization behaviour can be used, but that mainstream economists are unjustified in ignoring the contributions of our Keynesians because they have eschewed that method.

Finally, the mainstream attitude toward neo-Ricardians and Post Keynesians could be explained by an attempt by the economics profession to deny the truly revolutionary character of Keynes's theory. Keynes can be made sense of by assuming unemployment due to wage rigidity; unemployment equilibrium can be shown to exist, his multiplier works, and uncertainty and instability can be introduced. And if wages are in fact rigid, the behaviour of the economy would be very much the same (though with great differences in institutional detail) as the Post Keynesian and neo-Ricardian approaches. But the classical economists before him had realized that wage rigidity could cause unemployment (although they had not completely spelled out its implications for goods markets and aggregate demand). Keynes was well aware of this. He writes (JMK, VII, p. 257) that

the classical theory has been accustomed to rest the supposedly self-adjusting character of the economic system on an assumed fluidity of money wages; and, when there is rigidity, to lay on this rigidity the blame of maladjustment.

He makes it quite clear that he disagrees with the classical notion that a decline in the money wage would take the economy to full employment by inducing firms to hire more, since this ignored the macroeconomic effects which he analysed in detail. Thus Keynes viewed his theory to be quite revolutionary in not requiring wage rigidity to cause unemployment. The question arises as to why the profession would want to deny this revolutionary character.[5] There may be purely academic reasons such as the desire to maintain the corpus of standard neo-classical theory, which has learnt to incorporate wage-price rigidity (reconstituted reductionism, as Coddington (1983) calls it) without destroying the neo-classical edifice. But it may not be possible to introduce Post Keynesian and neo-Ricardian arguments within the general equilibrium system in an adequate manner without altering it beyond recognition, and to recognize the importance of these features could imply the abandonment of that apparatus.[6] Or it could be ideological. The removal of unemployment in the bastard Keynesian interpretation seems to require the cutting of wages and the destruction of unions, while in the Post Keynesian interpretation such changes would only aggravate unemployment. Thus which view one takes could depend on what position one takes on the question of class struggle.[7]

Whatever the reasons, strong pressures which load the dice in favour of mainstream economics have developed in the academic economics profession, and this makes it difficult for alternative views to proliferate and to be heard. These pressures are built by, and for, the orthodoxy to maintain its dominance in the profession and are reflected in ways by which academic work is judged in routine procedures such as journal refereeing and academic recruiting and tenuring. We can do no better than to quote Ward (1972) at length:[8]

The power inherent in this system of quality control within the economics profession is obviously very great. The discipline's censors occupy leading posts in economics departments at the major institutions . . . The lion's share of appointment and dismissal power has been vested in the departments themselves at these institutions. Any economist with serious hopes of obtaining a tenured position in one of these departments will soon be made aware of the criteria by which he is to be judged . . . the entire academic program, beginning usually at the undergraduate level but certainly at the graduate, consists of indoctrination in the ideas and techniques of the science . . . (Ward, 1972, pp. 29–30)

These inside instruments of control are accompanied by outside instruments exercised by members of the larger society. Probably the most important of these is control of funds for research and, to a lesser extent, teaching.

Consciences are not much troubled by such practices because economics has mixed its ideology into the subject so well that the ideologically unconventional usually appear to appointment committees to be scientifically incompetent (Ward, 1972, p. 250)

Despite these problems, the neo-Ricardians and the Post Keynesians should continue working on their research agendas. This is primarily because, as we have seen, they raise a variety of interesting and important issues that are typically glossed over by mainstream economists but which may prove to be the fundamental explanations of unemployment. It is also because their work provides the Keynesian revolution with a real chance, rather than relegating it to being only an elegant restatement of pre-Keynesian ideas. As Keynes prophetically wrote in the preface to his *General Theory*,

[t]hose who are strongly wedded to what I shall call 'the classical theory', will fluctuate, I expect, between a belief that I am quite wrong and a belief that I am saying nothing new. It is for others to determine if either of these or the third alternative is right. (JMK, VII, p. v)

If monetarist and rational expectation theorists are taken to be the group which now believes that Keynes is 'quite wrong', and mainstream Keynesians believing, in effect, that Keynes is 'saying nothing new', the neo-Ricardian Keynesians and the Post Keynesians seem to be most in a position to show, if at all, that 'the third alternative is right'.

NOTES

1. In fact Post Keynesians, broadly defined, have found the mathematical approach most suitable to the study of cyclical and growth issues. See, for example, Harris (1978), Taylor (1983), Marglin (1984), and Dutt (1989).
2. As noted by Eichner (1985, p. 151), '[i]t is less controversial to say what post-Keynesian theory is not than to say what it is [. . .] Post-Keynesian theory is not neoclassical theory'.
3. See Blinder (1987) and Rothschild (1988), for example, regarding microfoundations and Keynesian economics.
4. This is not to claim that the individual optimizing framework *necessarily* implies neglecting these issues; only that it has tended to divert attention away from them.

5. See Dutt and Amadeo (1989) for a fuller analysis of this question.
6. See E. Weintraub (1975) for a review of the relationship between general equilibrium theory and uncertainty.
7. It may be argued that mainstream Keynesian theory on wage rigidity, as discussed in chapter 2 above, does not say that wage rigidity is the result of labour union 'mischief' but could be the result of maximizing behaviour on the part of firms, as in efficiency wage theory. However, even this approach is based on some sort of a relation between efficiency and wages which may imply 'mischief' on the part of workers in the first place.
8. Cited by Robinson (1977).

References

Akerlof, George A. and Janet L. Yellen, eds., (1986). *Efficiency wage models of the labor market,* Cambridge: Cambridge University Press.

———— (1987). 'Rational Models of Irrational Behaviour', *American Economic Review,* Papers and Proceedings, May.

Amadeo, Edward (1987a). 'Multiplier Analysis', in John Eatwell, Murray Milgate and Peter Newman, eds., *The New Palgrave,* London: Macmillan.

———— (1987b). 'The Role of Capacity Utilization in Long-Period Analysis', *Political Economy,* 2(2).

———— (1988). 'Expectations in a Steady State Model of Capacity Utilization', *Political Economy,* 3(1).

———— (1989). *Keynes's Principle of Effective Demand,* Upleadon, Glos.: Edward Elgar.

Ambrosi, G. M. (1981). 'Keynes and the 45° cross', *Journal of Post Keynesian Economics.*

Arrow, Kenneth J and Frank H. Hahn (1971). *General Competitive Analysis,* San Francisco: Holden Day.

Asimakopulos, A. (1978). 'Keynesian Economics, Equilibrium and Time', *Canadian Journal of Economics,* 11(4), November.

———— (1982). Keynes' Theory of Effective Demand Revisited, *Australian Economic Papers,* June.

———— (1985). 'Keynes and Sraffa: Visions and Perspective', *Political Economy,* 1(2).

———— (1986). 'The Long-Period Employment' in the *General Theory', Journal of Post Keynesian Economics.*

Azariadis, Costas (1975). 'Implicit Contracts and Underemployment Equilibria', *Journal of Political Economy,* 83.

Backhouse, Roger (1988). 'The Value of Post Keynesian Economics: A neoclassical response to Harcourt and Hamouda', *Bulletin of Economic Research,* 40(1), 35–41.

Ball, R. J. (1964). *Inflation and the Theory of Money,* London: Allen and Unwin.

Baran, Paul and Paul Sweezy (1966). *Monopoly Capital,* New York: Monthly Review Press and Harmondsworth: Penguin.
Baumol, William J. (1952). 'The Transactions Demand for Cash: An Inventory Theoretic Approach', *Quarterly Journal of Economics,* 66, November, 545–56.
Bhaduri, Amit (1986). *Macroeconomics. The Dynamics of Commodity Production,* Armonk, New York: M. E. Sharpe.
Bharadwaj, Krishna (1983). 'On Effective Demand: Certain Critiques', in J. Kregel, ed., *Distribution, Effective Demand and International Economics Relations,* New York: St. Martin's.
———— (1985). 'Sraffa's Return to Classical Theory: Change and Equilibrium', *Political Economy* 1(2).
Bhattacharjea, Aditya (1987). 'Keynes and the Long-period Theory of Employment', *Cambridge Journal of Economics,* 11(3), September, 275–84.
Blanchard, O. J. and L. H. Summers (1987). 'Hysteresis in Unemployment', *European Economic Review,* 31, 288–95.
Blinder, Alan S. (1987). 'Keynes, Lucas, and Scientific Progress', *American Economic Review,* Papers and Proceedings.
Brown-Collier, E. (1985). 'Keynes' View of an Organic Universe: The Implications', *Review of Social Economy.*
Brothwell, J. F. (1987). 'On the Nature and Use of the Concept of the Marginal Physical Product in Post Keynesian Economics: a Comment', *Journal of Post Keynesian Economics,* Summer, 9(4), 496–501.
Carabelli, Anna (1985). 'J. M. Keynes on Cause, Chance and Possibility', in T. Lawson and H. Pesaran (1985).
———— (1988). *On Keynes's Method,* New York: St. Martin's Press.
Carvalho, Fernando (1984–5). 'Alternative Analyses of Short and Long Run in Post Keynesian Economics', *Journal of Post Keynesian Economics,* Winter.
———— (1988). 'Keynes on Probability, Uncertainty, and Decision Making', *Journal of Post Keynesian Economics,* Fall, 11(1), 66–81.
Casarosa, Carlo (1981). 'The Microfoundations of Keynes's Aggregate Supply and Expected Demand Analysis', *Economic Journal,* 91, March.
———— (1984). 'The Microfoundations of Keynes's Aggregate Supply and Expected Demand Analysis: a Reply', *Economic Journal,* 94.

Chick, Victoria (1983). *Macroeconomics After Keynes,* Cambridge, Massachusetts: MIT Press.

Ciccone, Roberto (1986). 'Accumulation and Capital Utilization: Some Critical Considerations on Joan Robinson's Theory of Distribution', *Political Economy,* 2(1).

Clower, Robert (1965). 'The Keynesian Counter-Revolution: A Theoretical Appraisal', in F. Hahn and F. Brechling, eds., *The Theory of Interest Rates,* London: Macmillan.

――――― (1967). 'A Reconsideration of the Microfoundations of Monetary Theory', *Western Economic Journal,* 6, 1-9.

Cochrane, J. L. (1971). 'Keynesian Probability and the General Theory', *Rivista Internazionale di Scienze Commerciali,* 18(4), April.

Coddington, Alan (1983). *'Keynesian Economics: The Search for First Principles,* London: Allen and Unwin.

Colander, David (1986). *Macroeconomics,* Glenville, Illinois: Scott, Foresman.

――――― (1988). 'The Evolution of Keynesian Economics: From Keynesian to New Classical to New Keynesian', in O. F. Hamouda and J. N. Smithin, eds., *Keynes and Public Policy After Fifty Years, Volume 1,* Washington Square, New York: New York University Press.

Committeri, Marco (1986). 'Some Comments on Recent Contributions on Capital Accumulation', *Political Economy,* 2(2).

Darity, William A. and Bobbie L. Horn (1983). 'Involuntary Unemployment Reconsidered', *Southern Economic Journal,* 49(3), 717-33.

Daugherty, M. R. (1942). 'The Currency/Banking Controversy: Part I', *Southern Economic Journal,* 9, October, 140-55.

――――― (1943). 'The Currency/Banking Controversy: Part II', *Southern Economic Journal,* 9, January, 241-51.

Davidson, Paul (1967). 'A Keynesian View of Patinkin's Theory of Employment', *Economic Journal,* June.

――――― (1972). *Money and the Real World,* London: Macmillan, New York: Wiley. 2nd ed., 1978.

――――― (1980). 'The Dual-Faceted Nature of the Keynesian Revolution: Money and Money Wages in Unemployment and Production Flow Prices', *Journal of Post Keynesian Economics,* 2(3), Spring.

――――― (1982). *International Money and the Real World,* London: Macmillan.

――――― (1982-3). 'Rational Expectations: A Fallacious Foundation for Studying a Crucial Decision-making Process', *Journal of Post Keynesian Economics,* 5(2), Winter.

_____ (1983). 'The Marginal Product Curve is not the Demand Curve for Labor and Lucas's Supply Curve for Labor is not the Supply Curve for Labor in the Real World', *Journal of Post Keynesian Economics,* Fall.

_____ (1984). 'Reviving Keynes's Revolution', *Journal of Post Keynesian Economics,* 6(4), Summer, 561–75.

_____ (1985). 'Liquidity and not Increasing Returns is the Ultimate Source of Unemployment Equilibrium', *Journal of Post Keynesian Economics.*

_____ (1986). 'A Scientific Definition of Uncertainty Forms the Basis For a Long-Run Non-Neutral Money System with Explicit Money Contracts', mimeo, Rutgers University.

_____ (1987a). 'Introduction: Lessons from Keynes's *General Theory*', *Journal of Post Keynesian Economics,* 10(1), Fall 1987.

_____ (1987b). 'A Technical Definition of Uncertainty and the Long Run Non-Neutrality of Money', unpublished, University of Tennessee, Knoxville, forthcoming, *Cambridge Journal of Economics.*

_____ and Eugene Smolensky (1964). *Aggregate Supply and Demand Analysis,* New York: Harper and Row.

de Jong, F. J. (1954a). 'Supply Functions in Keynesian Economics', *Economic Journal,* March.

_____ (1954b). 'Keynes and Supply Functions: A Rejoinder', *Economic Journal,* December.

_____ (1955). 'Keynes and Supply Functions: Second Rejoinder', *Economic Journal,* September.

_____ (1956). 'Keynes and Supply Functions: Third Rejoinder' and Final Observations , *Economic Journal,* September.

Diamond, Peter (1984). *A Search Equilibrium Approach to the Macro Foundations of Macroeconomics,* Cambridge, Mass.: MIT Press.

Dimand, Robert W. (1988). *The Origins of the Keynesian Revolution. The Development of Keynes' Theory of Employment and Output,* Aldershot: Edward Elgar.

Dornbusch, Rudiger and Stanley Fischer (1987). *Macroeconomics,* 4th ed., New York: McGraw-Hill.

Dow, Alexander and Sheila Dow (1985). 'Animal Spirits and Rationality', in Lawson and Pesaran (1986).

Dow, Sheila (1980). 'Methodological Morality in the Cambridge

Controversies', *Journal of Post Keynesian Economics,* 2(3), Spring.

———— (1985). *Macroeconomic Thought,* Oxford: Basil Blackwell.

———— (1986–7). 'Post Keynesian Monetary Theory for an Open Economy', *Journal of Post Keynesian Economics,* 9(2), Winter.

Drazen, Alan (1980). 'Recent Developments in Macroeconomic Disequilibrium Theory', *Econometrica,* March.

Dutt, Amitava Krishna (1984). 'Stagnation, Income Distribution and Monopoly Power', *Cambridge Journal of Economics,* 8(1).

———— (1985). 'A Keynesian Model of an Economy with a Perfectly Competitive Goods Market', Discussion Paper in Economics, No. 30, Florida International University, January.

———— (1986). 'On the Classical Dichotomy: Theory of Prices with Given Output and Distribution', mimeo, Florida International University.

———— (1986–7). 'Wage Rigidity and Unemployment: The Simple Diagrammatics of Two Views', *Journal of Post Keynesian Economics,* Winter.

———— (1987a). 'Keynes with a Perfectly Competitive Goods Market', *Australian Economic Papers,* December.

———— (1987b). 'Alternative Closures Again: A Comment on "Growth, Distribution and Inflation"', *Cambridge Journal of Economics,* 11(1), March.

———— (1988). 'Competition, Monopoly Power and the Prices of Production', *Thames Papers in Political Economy,* Autumn.

———— (1989). *Growth, Distribution and Uneven Development,* forthcoming, Cambridge: Cambridge University Press.

———— and Edward Amadeo (1989). 'Keynes's Dichotomy and Wage-Rigidity Keynesianism: A Puzzle in Keynesian Thought', in M. Blaug and D. Moggridge, eds., *Perspectives on the History of Economic Thought,* Upleadon, Glos.: Edward Elgar.

Eatwell, John (1977). 'Theories of Value, Output and Employment', *Thames Papers in Political Economy,* reprinted in Eatwell and Milgate (1983).

———— (1983). 'The Long Period Theory of Unemployment', *Cambridge Journal of Economics.*

———— and Murray Milgate (1983). 'Introduction', in Eatwell and Milgate (1983).

———— eds. (1983) *Keynes's Economics and the Theory of Value and Distribution,* London: Duckworth, and New York: Oxford University Press.

Eichner, Alfred S. (1976). *The Megacorp and Oligopoly,* Cambridge: Cambridge University Press.

_____ (1985). *Toward a New Economics,* Armonk, New York: M. E. Sharpe.

_____ (1987). 'McKenna and Zannoni on the Concept of Marginal Physical Product in Post Keynesian Economics', *Journal of Post Keynesian Economics,* Summer, 9(4), 502–6.

_____ and Jan A. Kregel (1975). 'An Essay on Post-Keynesian Theory: A New Paradigm in Economics', *Journal of Economic Literature,* 13(4), December.

Felderer, Bernhard and Stefan Homburg (1987). *Macroeconomics and New Macroeconomics,* Berlin: Springer–Verlag.

Fischer, Stanley (1977). 'Long-Term Contracts. Rational Expectations, and the Optimal Money Supply Rule', *Journal of Political Economy,* 85(1).

Foster, Gladys Parker (1986). 'The Endogeneity of Money and Keynes's General Theory', *Journal of Economic Issues,* XX, 4, December, 953–68.

Friedman, Milton (1974). 'Comments on the Critics', in R. J. Gordon, ed., *Milton Friedman's Monetary Framework,* Chicago: The University Press.

Garegnani, Pierangelo (1970). 'Heterogenous Capital, the Production Function and the Theory of Distribution', *Review of Economic Studies.*

_____ (1976). 'On a Change in the Notion of Equilibrium in Recent Work on Value and Distribution', in Eatwell and Milgate (1983).

_____ (1977). 'Changes and Comparisons: A Reply', mimeo, presented in the Joan Robinson memorial, Barnard College, New York.

_____ (1978–9). 'Notes on Consumption, Investment and Effective Demand', *Cambridge Journal of Economics,* reprinted in Eatwell and Milgate (1983).

_____ (1979). 'Reply to Joan Robinson', *Cambridge Journal of Economics,* reprinted in Eatwell and Milgate (1983).

_____ (1983). 'Two Routes to Effective Demand; Comment on Kregel', in J. A. Kregel, ed., *Distribution, Effective Demand and International Economic Relations,* St. Martin's New York.

_____ (1984). 'Value and Distribution in the Classical Economists and Marx', *Oxford Economic Papers.*

Goodwin, Richard M. (1951). 'The Non-linear Accelerator and the

Persistence of Business Cycles', *Econometrica*, 19(1), January, 1–17.

———— (1967). 'A Growth Cycle', in C. H. Feinstein, ed., *Socialism, Capitalism and Economic Growth*, Cambridge: Cambridge University Press.

———— (1982). *Essays in Economic Dynamics*, London: Macmillan.

———— and Lionello F. Punzo (1987). *The Dynamics of a Capitalist Economy*, Cambridge: The Polity Press.

Gram, Harvey and Vivian Walsh (1983). 'Joan Robinson's Economics in Retrospect', *Journal of Economic Literature*, 21(2), June.

Haberler, Gottfried (1946a). *Prosperity and Depression*, 3rd ed., Lake Success, New York: United Nations.

———— (1946b). 'The Place of The General Theory of Employment, Interest and Money in the History of Economic Thought', *Review of Economics and Statistics*, 28, November, 187–94. reprinted in Harris, ed. (1947), Chap XIV.

Hahn, Frank (1977). 'Keynesian Economics and General Equilibrium Theory: Reflections on Some Current Debates', G. C. Harcourt, ed., *Microeconomic Foundations of Macroeconomics*, London: Macmillan.

———— (1980). 'Monetarism and Economic Theory', *Economica*, 47, February, 1–17.

———— (1982). 'The Neo-Ricardians', *Cambridge Journal of Economics*.

———— (1987). 'Information, Dynamics and Equilibrium', *Scottish Journal of Political Economy*, 34(4), November.

———— and Robert Solow (1986). 'Is Wage Flexibility a Good Thing?', in W. Beckerman, ed., *Wage Rigidity and Unemployment*, Baltimore: The Johns Hopkins University Press.

Hamouda, O. F. and G. C. Harcourt (1988). 'Post Keynesianism: From Criticism to Coherence?', *Bulletin of Economic Research*, 40(1).

———— and J. N. Smithin (1988a). 'Some Remarks on "Uncertainty and Economic Analysis"', *Economic Journal*, 98, March, 159–64.

———— (1988b). 'Rational Behaviour and Deficient Foresight', *Eastern Economic Journal*, 14(3), July–September, 277–85.

Hansen, Alvin (1949). *Monetary Theory and Fiscal Policy*, New York: McGraw-Hill.

Harcourt, Geoffrey C. (1972). *Some Cambridge Controversies in the Theory of Capital*, Cambridge, Cambridge University Press.

_____ (1983). 'Keynes's College Bursar View of Investment: Comment on Kregel', in J. A. Kregel, ed., *Distribution, Effective Demand and International Economic Relations*, New York, St. Martin's.

_____ (1985). 'Post Keynesianism: Quite Wrong and/or Nothing New?', in P. Arestis and T. Skouras, eds., *Post Keynesian Economic Theory*, Sussex: Wheatsheaf Books; Armonk, New York: M. E. Sharpe.

_____ (1987a). 'Theoretical Methods and Unfinished Business', in David A. Reese, ed., *The Legacy of Keynes*, San Francisco: Harper & Row.

_____ (1987b). 'Post-Keynesian Economics', in J. Eatwell, M. Milgate and P. Newman, eds., *The New Palgrave*, London: Macmillan.

_____ and Peter Kenyon (1976). 'Pricing and the Investment Decision', *Kyklos*, 29, 449–77.

_____ and T. J. O'Shaughnessy (1985). 'Keynes's Unemployment Equilibrium: Some Insights from Joan Robinson, Pierro Sraffa and Richard Kahn', in G. C. Harcourt, ed., *Keynes and his Contemporaries*, London: Macmillan.

Harris, Donald J. (1978). *Capital Accumulation and Income Distribution*, Stanford: Stanford University Press.

Harris, Seymour E., ed. (1947). *The New Economics. Keynes' Influence on Theory and Public Policy*, New York: Alfred A. Knopf.

Harrod, Roy F. (1937). 'Mr Keynes and Traditional Theory', *Econometrica*, 5, January, repr. in Harris (1947).

_____ (1939). 'An Essay in Dynamic Theory', *Economic Journal*, 49, March, 14–33.

Hawtrey, R. G. (1954). 'Keynes and Supply Functions', *Economic Journal*, December.

_____ (1956). 'Keynes and Supply Functions', *Economic Journal*, September.

Heiner, R. A. (1983). 'The Origin of Predictable Behaviour', *American Economic Review*, 73, 560–95,

_____ (1985–6). 'Rational Expectations when Agents Imperfectly Use Information', *Journal of Post Keynesian Economics*, 8, 201–7.

Hicks, John R. (1937). 'Mr Keynes and the Classics: A Suggested Interpretation', *Econometrica*, 5, April, 147–59.

_____ (1950). *A Contribution to the Theory of the Trade Cycle*,

Oxford: Oxford University Press.

_____ (1976). 'Some Questions of Time in Economics', in A. M. Tang, et al., eds., *Evolution, Welfare and Time in Economics*, Lexington, Mass.: D. C. Heath & Co. Reprinted in Hicks (1982).

_____ (1979). *Causality in Economics*, Oxford: Basil Blackwell.

_____ (1980-1). 'IS-LM: An Explanation', *Journal of Post Keynesian Economics*, 3, Winter 139-54.

_____ (1982). *Money, Interest and Wages*, Cambridge, Mass.: Harvard University Press.

Hollander, Samuel (1987). *Classical Economics*, Oxford: Basil Blackwell.

Howitt, Peter (1986). 'Wage Flexibility and Unemployment', *Eastern Economic Journal*, 12(3), July-September.

Kahn, Richard (1959). 'Exercises in the Analysis of Growth', *Oxford Economic Papers*.

_____ (1977). 'Malinvaud on Keynes', *Cambridge Journal of Economics*, 1, 375-88, repr. in Eatwell and Milgate (1983).

_____ (1984). *The Making of Keynes' General Theory*, Cambridge University Press.

Kaldor, Nicholas (1940). 'A Model of the Trade Cycle', *Economic Journal*, 50, March, 78-92.

_____ (1957). 'A Model of Economic Growth', *Economic Journal*, December, repr. in Kaldor (1960).

_____ (1960). *Essays on Economic Stability and Growth*, Glencoe, Illinois: The Free Press.

_____ (1972). 'The Irrelevance of Equilibrium Economics', *Economic Journal*, 82, 1237-55.

_____ (1982). *The Scourge of Monetarism*, London: Oxford University Press.

_____ (1985). *Economics Without Equilibrium*, New York: Sharpe.

_____ and J. Trevithick (1981). 'A Keynesian Perspective on Money', *Lloyds Bank Review*, 139, January, 1-19.

Kalecki, Michal (1944). 'Professor Pigou on "The Classical Stationary State"': A Comment', *Economic Journal*, 54.

_____ (1954). *Theory of Economic Dynamics*, London: Allen & Unwin.

_____ (1971). *Selected Essays on the Dynamics of Capitalist Economies*, Cambridge: Cambridge University Press.

Keynes, John Maynard (1921). *Treatise on Probability*, London: Macmillan, repr. as JMK, VIII.

_____ (1936). *The General Theory of Employment, Interest and*

Money, London: Macmillan, repr. as JMK, VII.

_____ (1937a). 'The General Theory of Employment', *Quarterly Journal of Economics*, February, repr. in JMK, XIV.

_____ (1937b). 'Alternative Theories of the Interest Rate', *Economic Journal*, June, repr. in JMK, XIV.

_____ (1937c). 'The "Ex-Ante" Theory of the Rate of Interest', *Economic Journal*, December, repr. in JMK, XIV.

_____ (1971–82). *The Collected Writings of J. M. Keynes*, ed. Donald Moggridge, London: Macmillan, Vols V, VI, VII, VIII, X, XIII, XIV and XIX.

Kohn, Meir (1981). 'A Loanable Funds Theory of Unemployment and Monetary Disequilibrium', *American Economic Review*, 71(5), December, 859–79.

_____ (1986). 'Monetary Analysis, the Equilibrium Method, and Keynes's "General Theory" ', *Journal of Political Economy*, 94(6), 1191–224.

Kregel, Jan A. (1976). 'Economic Methodology in the Face of Uncertainty', *Economic Journal*, 86.

_____ (1983a). 'The Microfoundations of the "Generalisation of *The General Theory*" and "Bastard Keynesianism"': Keynes's Theory of Employment in the Long and Short Period', *Cambridge Journal of Economics*, 7, 343–61.

_____ (1983b). 'Effective Demand: Origins and Development of the Notion', in J. A. Kregel, ed., *Distribution, Effective Demand and International Economic Relations*, New York: St. Martin's.

_____ (1985). 'Sidney Weintraub's Macrofoundations of Microeconomics Without Money', *Journal of Post Keynesian Economics*, Summer, 7, 540–58.

_____ (1987). 'Keynes's Given Degree of Competition: Comment on McKenna and Zannoni', *Journal of Post Keynesian Economics*, Summer, 9(4), 490–5.

_____ (1988). 'The Multiplier and Liquidity Preference: Two Sides of the Theory of Effective Demand', in A. Barrere, ed., *The Foundations of Keynesian Analysis*, New York: St. Martin's.

Kreisler, Peter (1987). *Kalecki's Microanalysis: The Development of Kalecki's Analysis of Pricing and Distribution*, Cambridge: Cambridge University Press.

Kurihara, Kenneth K., ed. (1954). *Post Keynesian Economics*, New Brunswick, New Jersey: Rutgers University Press.

Kurz, Heinz D. (1985). 'Sraffa's Contribution to the Debate on Capital Theory', *Contributions to Political Economy*, 4.

Lange, Oscar (1938). 'The Rate of Interest and the Optimum Propensity to Consume', *Economica*, 5, February.

Lavoie, Marc (1984). 'The Endogenous Flow of Credit and the Post Keynesian Theory of Money', *Journal of Economic Issues*, XVIII (3), September, 771–97.

Lawson, Tony (1985). 'Uncertainty and Economic Analysis', *Economic Journal*, 95, December, 909–27.

_____ (1987). 'The Relative/Absolute Nature of Knowledge and Economic Analysis', *Economic Journal*, 97, December, 951–70.

_____ (1988). 'Probability and Uncertainty in Economic Analysis', *Journal of Post Keynesian Economics*, Fall, 11(1), 38–65.

_____ and Hashem Pesaran, eds., (1985). *Keynes' Economics – Methodological Issues*, Armonk, New York: M. E. Sharpe.

Leijonhufvud, Axel (1968). *On Keynesian Economics and the Economics of Keynes*, New York: Oxford University Press.

_____ (1974). 'Keynes' Employment Function, A Comment', *History of Political Economy*.

_____ (1981). *Information and Coordination*, New York and Oxford: Oxford University Press.

Lerner, Abba P. (1952). 'The Essential Properties of Interest and Money', *Quarterly Journal of Economics*, 46.

_____ and David C. Colander (1979). 'MAP – A Cure for Inflation', in D. Colander, ed., *Solutions to Inflation*, New York: Harcourt, Brace & Jovanovich.

Lindbeck, Assar and Dennis J. Snower (1987). 'Efficiency Wages Versus Insiders and Outsiders', *European Economic Review*.

McCallum, Bennett T. (1987). 'The Development of Keynesian Macroeconomics', *American Economic Review*, 77(2) Papers and Proceedings, May, 125–9.

McCombie, John S. L. (1985-6). 'Why Cutting Real Wages will not Necessarily Reduce Unemployment – Keynes and "the Postulates of the Classical Economics" ', *Journal of Post Keynesian Economics*, 8(2), Winter, 233–48.

McDonald, Ian M. and Robert M. Solow (1981). 'Wage Bargaining and Employment', *American Economic Review*, 71, December, 896–908.

McKenna, E. J. and D. C. Zannoni (1987). 'On the Nature and Use of the Concept of Marginal Physical Product in Post Keynesian Economics', *Journal of Post Keynesian Economics*, Summer, 9(4), 483–9.

Magnani, M. (1983). ' "Keynesian Fundamentalism": A Critique', in Eatwell and Milgate (1983).

Malinvaud, Edmond (1977). *The Theory of Unemployment Reconsidered*, Oxford: Basil Blackwell.

Marglin, Stephen (1984). *Growth, Distribution and Prices*, Cambridge, Mass.: Harvard University Press.

Marshall, Alfred (1890). *Principles of Economics*, 8th ed., London: Macmillan.

———— (1920). *Industry and Trade*, 3rd ed., London: Macmillan.

Marty, A. L. (1961). 'A Geometric Exposition of the Keynesian Supply Function', *Economic Journal*, September.

Meade, James (1937). 'A Simplified Model of Mr Keynes' System', *Review of Economic Studies*, 4, February, repr. in Harris (1947).

Meltzer, Alan H. (1981). 'Keynes' General Theory: A Different Perspective', *Journal of Economic Literature*, 19, March.

Milgate, Murray (1984). *Capital and Employment*, New York and London: Academic Press.

———— (1988). 'Money, Capital and Forced Saving', *Cambridge Journal of Economics*, 12(1), March, 43–54.

Millar, J. R. (1972). 'The Social Accounting Basis of Keynes' Aggregate Supply Function', *Economic Journal*, June.

Minsky, Hyman P. (1975). *John Maynard Keynes*, New York: Columbia University Press.

———— (1982). *Can 'It' Happen Again*, Armonk, New York: Sharpe.

———— (1986). *Stabilizing an Unstable Economy*, New Haven, Conn.: Yale University Press.

Mishan, E. J. (1964). 'The Demand for Labor in a Classical and Keynesian Framework', *Journal of Political Economy*, 72.

Modigliani, Franco (1944). 'Liquidity Preference and the Theory of Interest and Money', *Econometrica*, 12, January, 45–88.

———— (1986). *The Debate Over Stabilization Policy*, Cambridge: Cambridge University Press.

Moore, Basil J. (1979). 'The Endogenous Money Stock', *Journal of Post Keynesian Economics*, Fall, 49–70.

———— (1984). 'Contemporaneous Reserve Accounting: Can Reserves be Quantity-constrained?' *Journal of Post Keynesian Economics*, Fall, 7(1), 103–13.

———— (1986). 'How Credit Drives the Money Supply: The Significance of Institutional Developments', *Journal of Economic Issues*, XX(2), June, 443–54.

———— (1988a). 'The Endogenous Money Supply', *Journal of Post Keynesian Economics*, 10(3), Spring, 372–85.

_____ (1988b). *Horizontalists and Verticalists: The Macroeconomics of Credit Money*, Cambridge: Cambridge University Press.

Nell, Edward J. (1983). 'Keynes After Sraffa: The Essential Properties of Keynes's Theory of Interest and Money: Comment on Kregel', in J. A. Kregel, ed., *Distribution, Effective Demand and International Economic Relations*, New York: St. Martin's Press.

O'Donnell, R. M. (1982). 'Keynes: Philosophy and Economics – an approach to rationality and uncertainty', Ph.D. dissertation, University of Cambridge.

Panico, Carlo (1980). 'Marx's Analysis of the Relationship Between the Rate of Interest and the Rate of Profit', *Cambridge Journal of Economics*, repr. in Eatwell and Milgate (1983).

_____ (1985). 'Market Forces and the Relation Between the Rates of Interest and Profits', *Contributions to Political Economy*, 4, March.

_____ (1988). *Interest and Profit in the Theories of Value and Distribution*, London: Macmillan.

Parrinello, S. (1980). 'The Price Level Implicit in Keynes' Effective Demand', *Journal of Post Keynesian Economics*, Fall.

Pasinetti, Luigi (1962). 'Rate of Profit and Income Distribution in Relation to the Rate of Economic Growth', *Review of Economic Studies*, 29(4), October, pp. 267–79.

_____ (1974). 'The Economics of Effective Demand' in L. Pasinetti, *Growth and Income Distribution. Essays in Economic Theory*, Cambridge: Cambridge University Press.

_____ (1977). *Lectures on the Theory of Production*, New York: Columbia University Press.

_____ (1981). *Structural Change and Economic Growth*, Cambridge: Cambridge University Press.

Patinkin, Don (1965). *Money, Income and Prices*, 2nd ed., New York: Harper & Row.

_____ (1976). *Keynes' Monetary Thought*, Durham, North Carolina: Duke University Press.

_____ (1982). *Anticipations of the General Theory? and Other Essays on Keynes*, Chicago: Chicago University Press.

_____ and Leith, J. C., eds. (1977). *Keynes, Cambridge and the General Theory*, London: Macmillan.

Pigou, Arthur C. (1927). *Industrial Fluctuations*, London: Macmillan.

_____ (1933). *Theory of Unemployment*, London: Macmillan.

_____ (1936). 'Mr J. M. Keynes' *General Theory of Employment,*

Interest and Money', *Economica*, 3, May, 115-32.

———— (1943). 'The Classical Stationary State', *Economic Journal*, 53, December, 343-51.

Pivetti, Massimo (1985). 'On the Monetary Explanation of Distribution', *Political Economy*, 1(2).

———— (1988). 'Interest and Profit in Smith, Ricardo and Marx', *Political Economy*.

Presley, John R. (1986). 'J. M. Keynes and the Real Balance Effect', *The Manchester School*, March.

Roberts, D. L. (1978). 'Patinkin, Keynes, and Aggregate Supply and Demand Analysis', *History of Political Economy*, 10(4).

Robertson, D. H. (1955). 'Keynes and Supply Functions', *Economic Journal*, September.

———— (1956). 'Keynes and Supply Functions', *Economic Journal*, September.

———— (1957). *Lectures in Economic Principles*, Vol. I, London: Fontana.

Robinson, Joan (1937). *Essays in the Theory of Employment*, 2nd ed., 1947, Oxford: Blackwell.

———— (1956). *The Accumulation of Capital*, London: Macmillan.

———— (1962). *Essays in the Theory of Economic Growth*, New York: St Martin's.

———— (1974). 'History Versus Equilibrium', *Thames Papers in Political Economy*, repr. in *Collected Economic Papers*, Vol. V, Cambridge, Mass.: MIT Press, 1980.

———— (1977). 'What Are the Questions', *Journal of Economic Literature*, December, repr. in *Collected Economic Papers*, Vol. V, Cambridge, Mass.: MIT Press, 1980.

———— (1978). 'Keynes and Ricardo', *Journal of Post Keynesian Economics*, repr. in *Collected Economic Papers*, Vol V. Cambridge, Mass.: MIT Press, 1980.

Rotheim, Roy J. (1988). 'Keynes and the Language of Probability and Uncertainty', *Journal of Post Keynesian Economics*, Fall, 11(1), 82-99.

Rothschild, Kurt W. (1988). 'Micro-Foundations, Ad Hocery, and Keynesian Theory', *Atlantic Economy Journal*, June, 16(2), 12-21.

Rousseas, Stephen (1986). *Post Keynesian Monetary Economics*, Armonk, New York: M. E. Sharpe.

Samuelson, Paul A. (1939). 'Interaction Between the Multiplier Analysis and the Principle of Acceleration', *Review of Econ-*

omics and Statistics, 31, May, 75-8.

Sawyer, Malcolm (1985). *The Economics of Michal Kalecki*, London: Macmillan.

Schlesinger, J. R. (1956). 'After Twenty Years: The General Theory', *Quarterly Journal of Economics*, November, 581-603.

Shackle, G. L. S. (1938). *Expectations, Investment and Income*, London: Macmillan.

_____ (1955). *Uncertainty and Economics*, Cambridge: Cambridge University Press.

_____ (1967). *The Years of High Theory*, Cambridge: Cambridge University Press.

_____ (1968). *A Scheme of Economic Theory*, Cambridge: Cambridge University Press.

_____ (1972). *Epistemics and Economics*, Cambridge: Cambridge University Press.

_____ (1982). 'Sir John Hicks' "IS-LM: An Explanation": A Comment', *Journal of Post Keynesian Economics*, 4(3), Spring.

_____ (1984). 'General Thought-Schemes and the Economist', *Thames Papers in Political Economy*, Autumn.

Shapiro, Nina (1978). 'Keynes and Equilibrium Economics', *Australian Economic Papers*, 17, December.

Skott, Peter (1989). 'Effective Demand, Class Struggle and Cyclical Growth', *International Economic Review*, forthcoming.

Solow, Robert M. (1979). 'Alternative Approaches to Macroeconomic Theory: A Partial View', *Canadian Journal of Economics*, 12(3), August.

_____ (1984). 'Mr Hicks and the Classics', *Oxford Economic Papers*, November, 13-25.

_____ (1985). 'Economic History and Economics', *American Economic Review* - Papers and Proceedings, 75(2), May.

_____ (1986). *Consequences of Unemployment Equilibrium*, forthcoming (tentative title), Oxford: Basil Blackwell.

Sraffa, Piero (1932). 'Dr Hayek on Money and Capital', *Economic Journal*, 42, March.

_____ (1960). *Production of Commodities by Means of Commodities*, Cambridge: Cambridge University Press.

Steindl, Josef (1952). *Maturity and Stagnation in American Capitalism*, Oxford: Blackwell.

Stohs, M. (1980). ' "Uncertainty" in Keynes' General Theory', *History of Political Economy*, 12(3), Autumn.

Tarshis, Lorie (1939). 'The Determination of Labour Income', unpublished Ph. D. dissertation, University of Cambridge.

_____ (1947). *The Elements of Economics. An Introduction to the Theory of Price and Employment*, Boston: Houghton Mifflin Co.

_____ (1948). 'An Exposition of Keynesian Economics', *American Economic Review*, 38, 261-91.

_____ (1979). 'The Aggregate Supply Function in Keynes's "General Theory" ', in M. J. Boskin, ed., *Economics and Human Welfare*, New York and London: Academic Press.

_____ (1980). 'Post-Keynesian Economics: A Promise that Bounced?', *American Economic Review*, 70(2), May.

Taylor, Lance (1983). *Structuralist Macroeconomics*, New York: Basic Books.

Termini, V. (1981). 'Logical, Mechanical and Historical Time in Economics', *Economic Notes*, 10(3), 58-104.

Tobin, James A. (1958). 'Liquidity Preference as Behaviour Towards Risk', *Review of Economic Studies*, 25, February, 65-86.

_____ (1975). 'Keynesian Models of Recession and Depression', *American Economic Review*, 65, Papers and Proceedings, 195-202.

_____ (1980). *Asset Accumulation and Economic Activity*, Chicago: Chicago University Press.

Torr, C. S. W. (1981). 'Microfoundations of Keynes's Point of Effective Demand', *South African Journal of Economics*, 49(4).

_____ (1984). 'The Microfoundations of Keynes's Aggregate Supply and Expected Demand Analysis: A Comment', *Economic Journal*, 94.

Townshend, Hugh (1937). 'Liquidity Premium and the Theory of Value', *Economic Journal*, 47(1), March.

Trevithick, J. (1976). 'Money Wage Inflexibility and the Keynesian Labour Supply Function', *Economic Journal*, 86.

Vianello, F. (1985). 'The Pace of Accumulation', *Political Economy*, 1(1).

Ward, Benjamin (1972). *What's Wrong with Economics*, New York: Basic Books.

Weintraub, E. Roy (1974). 'Keynes' Employment Function: Comment', *History of Political Economy*.

_____ (1975). 'Uncertainty and the Keynesian Revolution', *History of Political Economy*, 7.

_____ (1979). *Microfoundations*, Cambridge: Cambridge University Press.

_____ (1985). *General Equilibrium Analysis*, Cambridge: Cambridge University Press.

Weintraub, Sidney (1958). *An Approach to the Theory of Income Distribution*, Philadelphia: Chilton.

―――― (1978a). *Capitalism's Inflation and Unemployment Crisis*, Boston: Addison Wesley.

―――― (1978b). *Keynes, Keynesians and Monetarists*, Philadelphia: University of Pennsylvania Press.

Weitzman, Martin (1982). 'Increasing Returns and the Foundations of Unemployment Theory', *Economic Journal*, December.

―――― (1985). 'The Simple Macroeconomics of Profit Sharing', *American Economic Review*, December.

Wells, Paul (1960). 'Keynes' Aggregate Supply Function: A Suggested Interpretation', *Economic Journal*, September.

―――― (1962). 'Aggregate Supply and Demand: An Explanation of Chapter III of the General Theory', *Canadian Journal of Economics and Political Science*, November.

―――― (1978). 'In Review of Keynes', *Cambridge Journal of Economics*, 2.

―――― (1979a). 'Modigliani on Flexible Wages and Prices', *Journal of Post Keynesian Economics*.

―――― (1979b). 'Money and the Money Wage Rate', in M. J. Boskin, ed., *Economics and Human Welfare*, New York and London: Academic Press.

Winslow, E. (1986). 'Human Logic and Keynes's Economics', *Eastern Economic Journal*, 12, 413–30.

Wood, Adrian (1975). *A Theory of Profits*, Cambridge: Cambridge University Press.

Wray, Larry Randall (1988). 'Profit Expectations and the Investment-Saving Relation', *Journal of Post Keynesian Economics*, Fall, 11(1), 131–47.

Yellen, Janet L. (1980). 'On Keynesian Economics and the Economics of the Post-Keynesians', *American Economic Review*, 70(2), May.

Young, Warren (1987). *Interpreting Mr Keynes. The IS–LM Enigma*, Cambridge: Polity Press and Boulder, Colorado: Westview Press.

Index

This book may be kept